Books by Malcolm Boyd

Crisis in Communication
On the Battle Lines (Edited by Malcolm Boyd)
Are You Running With Me, Jesus?
Malcolm Boyd's Book of Days

MALCOLM BOYD'S
BOOK OF DAYS

Heinemann · SCM Press Ltd London

William Heinemann Ltd · SCM Press Ltd

First published in Great Britain 1968

Copyright © 1968 by Malcolm Boyd

434 08402 6 (hardback)
434 08403 4 (paperback)

The author is grateful to the following publishers for permission to reprint from their works: Astor-Honor, Inc. for *The Shame of the Nation*, by Philip M. Stern and George de Vincent. Copyright © 1965 by Philip M. Stern and George de Vincent; Faber & Faber Ltd. for "For the Time Being", by W. H. Auden, reprinted from *The Collected Poetry of W. H. Auden*; and for *Markings*, by Dag Hammarskjold, Copyright © by Alfred A. Knopf, Inc., and Faber & Faber Ltd; Harper & Row Publishers for *Dark Ghetto*, by Kenneth B. Clark; Holt, Rinehart & Winston, Inc. for *The Holocaust*, by Alexander Donat, Copyright © 1963, 1965 by Alexander Donat; and for *My People is the Enemy*, by William Stringfellow, Copyright © 1964 by William Stringfellow; and Morehouse-Barlow Co., Inc. for *The Hunger, the Thirst* and *If I Go Down to Hell*, by Malcolm Boyd; and Random House Inc. for *Mississippi Black Paper*. Copyright © 1965 by Misseduc Foundation Inc.

Printed in Great Britain by Cox & Wyman Ltd,
London, Fakenham and Reading

To my mother BEATRICE BOYD
in the seventieth year of her days

Preface

Minutes and hours, people and places, family
problems and human revolutions, work and leisure,
straws of life and confrontation of moral issues, joy
and pain, are the stuff making up a book of days. Of
course, the days extend into weeks, then months
and years. It is the grist of life which absorbs us.

A book of days is inescapably a book of views. The
views here sometimes belong to other people, yet
basically they must reflect one man – living his life,
observing (and participating in) his times, breathing
the air of his age, and sharing experiences with others
who are as human as he knows himself to be. *This*
is a book of days.

MALCOLM BOYD

Washington D.C.
February, 1968

JANUARY

1 *That Wall:*

is it in my way or is it protecting me?

2 *Why Won't Our Leaders Lead Us?*

Are they afraid?
Have they sold us out for some old silver or new invest-
ments?
Are they, perhaps, trapped in double-standard ethics and
price tags?
Have they been told what it may *cost* if they lead us?
Must the charade go on, the empty ritual of leadership, the
prophetic vacuum, the implicit hypocrisy (old, old wisdom
keeps it always implicit), the boat which rots but does not
rock?
But we want moral leadership. Honesty. Guts. We cannot
accept leaders in name only.
Why won't our leaders lead us?

3 *Comments After, or Before, the Fall*

On a rainy night in New York City, in the period of Enlight-
enment marked by America's Solution to the Racial Problem,
two men (*this is a true story*) were walking downtown and (*I
swear it happened*) one was heard to remark (*yes*) to the other
(*it was in January*): 'I want you to understand, I've got nothing,
absolutely nothing, against the Negro, but.'

4 *I am up to My Elbows in Hell*

– so are my people. I try to let God love them through me.
Do they know they are in Hell? Of what do I need preach: the

I

reality of Hell they will not face, or the reality of Love they do not know? They are 'middle class'. They are lonely. They have compromised. They are afraid. They have pleasures – little joy. Me too.

Letter from a clergyman

5

I loved you in a desperate, fresh, urgent way once. You know this. You remade my world, as if it had been clay. I could live in the new world you let me see. But I could do this only when I was with you. When I could not be with you, that world was just a dream for me. Do you understand this?

When we could no longer be together, and it was necessary for us to become separated (worlds away), I couldn't walk back into the old world I knew. I couldn't function in the one you had shown (given?) me.

So there had to be a new one. This is what I have never been able to share with you or tell you about. That new world. And what can I say about it now that will really describe it, or myself in it?

The new world held a number of fulfilments for me. It was a terrain I had to discover and explore by myself. I had no maps and often no sense of direction. I trusted certain people who hurt me when they betrayed this trust. (Of course, I must have hurt and betrayed them too.) Yet I knew there must be risks in everything, especially in relationships.

We have lived, holding one another in an arrested state of being. I could only assume the crises and decisions, the sadnesses and fulfilments, within your life and never know them. But I wanted to know them. It was the desire for this knowing which I had to relinquish. I finally did.

I love you. What that means, now, for us, I cannot be sure. It is just that I speak to you from my heart. What is my heart? It is where I feel the most tender things, where my life is

2

touched by an ultimate sensitivity. Here, in my heart, I love you. I feel your life tenderly. I am rawly sensitive to your existence. I am not whole without you, so have never been whole.

It is foolish, though, to speak of wholeness. Everyone I know is somehow fragmented, a creature of memory, fulfilled and not fulfilled, torn into pieces of time and suddenly, in short moments, glued together. So I am not feeling sorry for myself. In fact, I am aware how, if our lives had not been separated, there would not have been this strange wholeness of which I am now speaking.

It is just that there would have seemed to be more wholeness. There would, indeed, have been *more* wholeness. So there it is.

6

The tiny children do not cry out in pain; if they make any sound it is a soft moaning; they twist their wounded bodies in silence. In the cot by the door is a child burned by napalm. He is seven years old, the size of a four-year-old of ours. His face and back and bottom and one hand were burned. A little piece of something like cheesecloth covers his body; it seems that any weight would be intolerable, but so is air. His hand is burned, stretched out like a starfish; the napalmed skin on the little body looks like bloody hardened meat in a butcher's shop. ('We always get the napalm cases in batches,' the doctor had said. And there's white phosphorus too and it's worse because it goes on gnawing at flesh like rat's teeth, gnawing to the bone.) An old man, nearly blind with a cataract, was tending this burned child, his grandson. The napalm bombs fell a week ago on their hamlet, he carried the child to the nearest town, and they were flown here by helicopter. The child cried with pain all that week, but today he is better, he is not crying, only twisting his body to try to find some way to lie that does not hurt him.

From 'Vietnam: A New Kind of War' by Martha Gellhorn

7 Student Questions

Q: Father Boyd, how can you answer people who say, 'Prove that there is a God?'

Father Boyd: I don't know. The question bores me. I don't think it is important. I don't usually answer it. I mean, there are real problems in the world. People are starving to death, and blacks and whites aren't getting along, and there is a population explosion, and we're dropping napalm on villages in Asia. . . . I think a lot of people enjoy sitting around discussing these academic questions, like how many angels are dancing on the head of a needle, or is there a God . . . but they're not my questions . . . I was an atheist all through college. Nobody giving me all these answers would have meant anything to me.

Q: You do believe in God, don't you?

Father Boyd: I do, yes. But the only way anyone else is going to be affected by it is if I show in my life that I do, and, of course, I think then we need to explore what that means. I mean, to me God is the spirit of relationship rather than brokenness, involvement rather than drop out or conk out . . .

Q: Father Boyd, do you believe Jesus is the true son of God?

Father Boyd: What are you talking about? This is a cliché to me. It's sort of like accepting this cliché Jesus Christ is your personal lord and saviour. Well, people want to sort of break it down and be cool about it. I mean, how would you define it? . . . I don't think he was a nice man in any event. He was sort of sweaty. He no doubt smelled. He upset the religious establishment and they nailed him up as a common

4

criminal, you know. But, a lot of people who go to church, I don't think would probably like to have him for dinner. No, for me there is a uniqueness. The whole meaning of Jesus for me is that instead of being in a cloud over Las Vegas or something, God radically got involved in life and isn't remote . . . this is not simply another guy, but I think in the sense of Jesus we grasp this involvement of God in our lives.

Q: What should be the role of church in the world today?

Father Boyd: Well, to get out of the real estate business would help, and a few less society weddings I think would be helpful. I still say Sunday School made me an atheist . . . . To get closer to people, not to rest on privilege, but to get involved in responsibilities to serve. You see, we have all these buildings, and they're locked up, many of them, except for an hour a week when the people dress up in a rather odd way and come in and involve themselves, frequently, I think, in an idolatry, worshipping religion rather than God, and then they come out of the building and that's that. Well now, I have a feeling that maybe they won't have the buildings but the clergymen are going to be working alongside of the people, we're going to see some rather fundamental changes. And I think when and if this happens, the church that is people rather than an office somewhere, or a cathedral, is going to be involved more in the problems of people and society.

From the television programme 'Youth Wants to Know'

8 *What Should a Boy Do?*

when a girl invites him to her house at night and her parents are not home? How far should a boy let a girl go?

Letter from a teen-age boy

9

A light bulb just burned out in my room. There was an almost imperceptible pop for a second, then it was gone.

I wonder how many people in the world died in this same moment? How many babies were born? How many light bulbs burned out? Are lights turned on or off – what time is it – in São Paulo, Cairo, Copenhagen, New Delhi, Tel Aviv, Peking, Sydney and Accra?

10

The stairway smelled of piss.

The smells inside the tenement – number 18, 342 East 100th Street, Manhattan – were somewhat more ambiguous. They were a suffocating mixture of rotting food, rancid mattresses, dead rodents, dirt, and the stale odours of human life.

This was to be home. It had been home before: for a family of eight – five kids, three adults. Some of their belongings had been left behind. Some of their life had, too.

The place, altogether, was about 25 × 12 feet, with a wall separating the kitchen section from the rest. In the kitchen was a bath, a tiny, rusty sink, a refrigerator that didn't work, and an ancient gas range. In one corner was a toilet with a bowl without a seat. Water dripped perpetually from the box above the bowl. The other room was filled with beds: two double-decker military cots, and a big ugly convertible sofa. There wasn't room for anything else. The walls and ceilings were mostly holes and patches and peeling paint, sheltering legions of cockroaches.

This was to be my home.

I wondered, for a moment, why.

Then I remembered that this was the sort of place in which

most people live, in most of the world, for most of the time. This or something worse.

Then I was home.

From 'My People Is the Enemy' by William Stringfellow

11 *My Brother*

doesn't want a keeper. He wants a brother.

12 *Apart-ment*

It's moving day again. As a boy the world I knew was the world of city apartments. Life was carried on high up in a building, so that one could not run out of doors on to a lawn or into a yard; it was bound by elevators and stairways and people one never spoke to. Apart-ment. Being apart, and so close together; not communicating, yet hearing sounds through the walls.

Did we move more because we lived in apartments? Moving day meant up and down in elevators, the moving man taking everything down. The walls bare, the funny-looking empty rooms, the rugs up and the pictures down, I suddenly realized this was my home, *my home*. It was time to go, but I hadn't even left a mark on my home – not a mark.

Yet what mark could I have left there but my breath on the walls, my footsteps on the floors, my life in the rooms? And had I not been given something to take away with me and puzzle over, this easygoing informal community amid the anonymity? There were possibilities for sharing with others that I had let slip because I had felt both attracted and threatened.

It's moving day again: an opportunity for new people, new choices.

To a King in an old castle:

All I can see are ruins on a hill, but I know you're still around – handing out orders, parading down mirrored hallways in your wig, arranging discreetly public dates with those very fashionable courtesans, preparing your eldest son for kingship, marrying off a daughter to a duke, flogging a rebellious slave to death, and, in every way, letting everybody know that God's in his heaven and all's right with his world.

Incidentally, you'd better perfume that wig again; it's smelling rather strong.

14 *At the Flicks:* The Bible

Confronted by yet another (and always the same) Hollywood biblical spectacular – complete with battles, bedrooms and bedlam – one wonders: What will God *do*?

15 *Unless*

we have become free to die, we are not yet free to live.

16

A sign on an apartment house entrance:
THIS DOOR OPENS AT 6 A.M.
Why? Who made this decision? When does the door *close*? Why? Who made *that* decision? (Maybe it's time we started organizing around here.)

17

One day when we came back from work, we saw three gallows rearing up in the assembly place, three black crows. Roll call. SS all around us, machine guns trained; the traditional ceremony. Three victims in chains – and one of them, the little servant, the sad-eyed angel.

The SS seemed more preoccupied, more disturbed than usual. To hang a young boy in front of thousands of spectators was no light matter. The head of the camp read the verdict. All eyes were on the child. He was lividly pale, almost calm, biting his lips. The gallows threw its shadow over him. . . .

The three victims mounted together on to the chairs.

The three necks were placed at the same moment within the nooses.

'Long live liberty!' cried the two adults.

But the child was silent.

'Where is God? Where is He?' someone behind me asked.

At a sign from the head of the camp, the three chairs tipped over. . . .

I heard a voice within me answer . . . :

'Where is He? Here He is – He is hanging on this gallows . . .'

From 'Night' by Elie Wiesel

18

I am groping – as all men searching for purpose are – but I find it difficult to bring things to the surface. I'm afraid. It's not the fear of darkness – but, perhaps, the fear of not being honest. When I say I am an idealist – what are my ideals? I want to do something, to be something – no, that's not it, damn it!

Why am I here? Sometimes I think I have the answer, then its meaning slips away from me. It's got something to do with being in the chain of history and life.

The human heart is capable of cruelty and kindness. I often forget that cruelty stems from the same source as kindness. But, why? Am I capable of such cruelty? I hope not, and fear so.

What are my fears and what are my ideals? Do I really 'love'

9

humanity – but some are so ugly. Am I ugly, too? The masses are stupid – but am I not one of the masses?

I've always been afraid of telling anyone what I've been thinking. I must open up. I'm crying. Please, listen.

Letter from a university student

19 *The Compulsive Need*

to feel a part of everything and yet be out of it all. I need a pair of dark glasses. Shades make me feel shut away, cool, separate. They even make me feel important, mysterious (a film star, a foreign dignitary?). They grant me identity by seeming to obscure it.

What style of rims do I want to project what image?

20 *It Is Only a Flower*

or, rather, it is a flower.

It is crimson, a bit scrawny (for this flower is naked against the white wall, separated from others in a bouquet); it rests in a green vase on a shelf in my room. It is not *my* room; I am visiting and will be here briefly. The flower and I share this condition. It sends warmth to me from its place on the shelf. In a drab, though acceptably contemporary room, the flower symbolizes all of beauty.

The flower and I share a moment, a mutual awareness (this must be so), time, space, living and dying.

21 *I'll Never Forget the Day My Mother Told Me I Was Red*

I had always thought she was purple and my father was orange, so this left me feeling suddenly quite stranded and isolated. A terrible loneliness and sadness swept over me. Why did I have to be red? Wouldn't this make me different from other people?

But my mother explained how she and my father were *really* red, only with variations. So, she said, were almost two tenths of everybody. This made me feel better. After all, two tenths is pretty respectable.

I couldn't ever forget after that, though, how I'm red. This bugged me because I couldn't figure it out. Why was it? To complicate things, I noticed how some people went out of their way to be nice to me *because* I am red, and some other people were mean to me for the same reason.

In fact, something ugly happened to me one day. Someone shouted 'rigger' at me. This is mean because it's meant to be. I didn't know until later that bigots shout 'bigger' at blue people, 'yigger' at yellows and 'gigger' at greens. Good Lord, things were becoming really complicated. Whites were called 'wiggers' and blacks should have been called 'biggers' but were called 'niggers' instead. I could never understand why.

Later, I learned that there are subtle variations on all these names. Some people deliberately say 'rigra,' 'bigra', 'yigra,' 'wigra' and 'nigra.'

My own family seemed to be what they called integrated, what with purple and orange, but they still made a big point of my being sent to an integrated school. What a splash! Blues were all over the place, then there were lots of yellows and greens. I always had a hard time focusing on whites – one minute they seemed to be there, the next minute you knew they weren't, because it was only the sunlight shining on a white-painted wall. Just as soon as I seemed to be striking up a friendship with a white, he'd sort of drift away. He was gone. I'd look and look, but I could never exactly locate him. I had one black friend. He was okay but I gave up on him because I decided I wanted more colour in my close associates.

I went away to an integrated college and started dating a green. I had to get used to her greenness. Her green hair probably bothered me the most, and, when she'd cry, it looked like emeralds. But I loved her. My mother and father didn't want me to date her. They asked me, 'Can't you find someone of your own kind to love?' Her parents were angry and refused to allow me inside their house. We got along okay, anyway, until green consciousness hit. The greens were supposed to concentrate on being green. Green was great and everything else was bad, but red was the worst. My girl was even dying her hair *greener*. I tried some green cream but it didn't work, and that seemed to make her mad, and then she broke up with me. I hear she joined some green-nationalist group.

This made me decide maybe I needed to belong to some kind of red-nationalist group. But I'm still looking for enough reds. It's sort of hung me up.

22 *The establishment*

that prays together rules together.

23

We've got a nice little problem here – mainly required church has made religion a farce and most of us in the student body feel that required services should be curtailed.

Our policy in regard to church is to ignore the chaplain or whoever is giving the service (Morning Prayer or Holy Communion on Holy Days).

A prayer is said before every meal in the dining hall. A triangle is struck, a microphone clicks on. Talking stops. 'Bless O Lord' (glasses turn over, dishes slide up and down the table) 'this food to our use' (pitchers pour instant iced tea into 800 glasses) 'and us to Thy service and make us ever mindful of the needs of others' (chairs slide out from the table) 'in Christ's name we pray. Amen' (accompaniment of chairs sliding in).

Letter from a student attending a church-related college

24

I'm surprised how really hurt I am.

I thought I was too sophisticated to be. And, after all, it was merely a routine business matter.

So, suddenly, in an exceptionally bright moment of truth, I realized I was being treated as a 'thing', as a business commodity or a cog in an economic success story, rather than as a person.

The shades flew up, light was pouring in and, in that moment of insight, I realized I had been fooling myself. I had thought that, underneath the dollars and brisk business talk, I was cared for as myself. But I was just being fattened for exhibition at the fair, and, if a bidder could go high enough, the kill.

How to survive when impersonality jumps out from behind smiling masks and announces this is the way it is?

25

The cure for loneliness is solitude.

From 'If I Were Sixteen Today' by Marianne Moore

26 *Brotherhood Nights*

Tonight is the annual community Brotherhood dinner.

Let's see: We must have a rabbi, a priest *and* a minister. (Why can't the ecumenical movement move faster?) That means one invocation and two benedictions, or two invocations and one benediction.

For our guest speaker, we want a BIG NAME who can

DRAW A CROWD (at $7.50 per head, to be exact; we've got to make dough tonight). Don't let the speaker be controversial. Yet, of course, he must *appear* to be – that is, he must speak emotionally about safe, liberal causes.

We won't pay the speaker. We're appealing to his interest in 'good causes' (ours). This means the money goes to *our* causes, not *his*.

He should speak no longer than thirty minutes. After all that food and drink, he'll have to fight to keep us awake! (But not too wide awake.) And, if the speaker should get out of line – if he's not content to be a one-night-stand scapegoat for pulling in dough via his big name, but should want to say something controversial – CRUCIFY HIM! If he's too honest, NAIL HIM UP! If he gives us the facts, CALL HIM A PHONY, A PHONY, A PHONY, A PHONY, A PHONY! Goddamnit, don't let him come in here and tell *us* the truth as he sees it.

IT'S BROTHERHOOD NIGHT!

27 *A Prayer*

Everything is in a shambles, Jesus.

Everybody is hurt, including me. There doesn't seem to be any real honest communication between anybody at all here, despite the endless talking about it.

It's just that we all seem to be complete strangers to each other. This, despite everything we've said and done together. It's all been blown to pieces.

People smiled but bitched behind each other's backs. We wouldn't say anything out in the open about a problem, but were up half the night talking about each other with suspicion and guilt in twos and threes.

So it's out now. I don't know if it's better or worse than before. I only know I couldn't go on with it the other way. So

I've given you a new mess to deal with, while claiming to serve and love you. This is what drives me to despair or a feeling of madness or complete exhaustion about everything.

In a few minutes I'll go downstairs and put on at least a small mask, and try, with the others, to carry on.

Please be downstairs with us, Lord. Please be upstairs with me now. Please unravel what is incomprehensibly tight. Please, somehow, speak to us all at once, yet to each of us alone, and tell us how to love each other enough so that we can express our love of you.

28

He told me, 'Malcolm, you ought to be thinking about a career. Have you been giving it thought?'

The truth is, I hadn't. I never have figured out why I told him, 'Well, yes, sir, I've been thinking I'd like to be a lawyer.' Lansing certainly had no Negro lawyers – or doctors either – in those days, to hold up an image I might have aspired to. All I really know for certain was that a lawyer didn't wash dishes, as I was doing.

Mr Ostrowski looked surprised, I remember, and leaned back in his chair and clasped his hands behind his head. He kind of half-smiled and said, 'Malcolm, one of life's first needs is for us to be realistic. Don't misunderstand me, now. We all here like you, you know that. But you've got to be realistic about being a nigger. A lawyer – that's no realistic goal for a nigger. You need to think about something you *can* be. You're good with your hands – making things. Everybody admires your carpentry shop work. Why don't you plan on carpentry? People like you as a person – you'd get all kinds of work.'

From 'The Autobiography of Malcolm X'

A Great Star, swathed in furs and glistening in jewels, is being escorted from her shiny black limousine towards the entrance of the grand hotel.

It is a climactic scene in the movie. Actually, she is an imperial princess but is posing as a spy. Her lover, the peasant leader (who is really a grand duke), is waiting for her by the hotel entrance. The chief of the secret police, elegantly attired in a full-dress uniform, waits inside under the crystal chandelier to arrest her.

What will happen to the princess? Will she elude arrest and elope with her lover (with both of them returning to her kingdom to reign), be executed at dawn by a firing squad, or live long enough to be sliced into neat sequences between beer commercials?

30 *Breakfast Revolution*

NOT two eggs, sunny-side up, with toast and bacon;
NOT a bowl of oatmeal or cornflakes;
NOT hotcakes with syrup;
But a toasted bagel, Nova Scotia salmon, cream cheese, and
TWO SLICES OF RAW, WET ONION – *THICK* SLICES.

31 *Imperfect World*

The world is white. I see no contrasts in it. It is a whipped-cream, romantic morning scene after a night's snowfall.

Winged angels, singing, yet without their trumpets which they presumably left at home, fly overhead. The newspaper is white (although its black print seems in bad taste). My coffee would be black unless I added cream to it – *add cream, add cream* – for it must immediately be made as white as possible. I see a quite-out-of-place red chair; why hasn't it been reup-holstered in a white weave?

Ah, South Africa. *It* could be all white, too, if genocide could progress adequately and without silly moral hangups and a godawful religious legacy of guilt. Yet, it doesn't snow there the year round, does it? This is so disappointing, I could cry.

Observing my room, I study a glaringly inexcusably im-perfect world: a brown table, a yellow magazine cover, an orange vase (without flowers, thank God), a red spine on a white book (those New York Jewish publishers are danger-ously leftish), a blue cup, a coloured (I shudder) telephone. ... Can there be perfection, and pure whiteness, *only* in heaven and God's kingdom?

Ahh. My teeth. My teeth are beautifully, shiningly, glisten-ingly, dazzlingly, white. I share this with the singing angels overhead. (But why *did* they leave their trumpets at home?)

FEBRUARY

1 *A Car May Crash*

I remember how, late one night, I drove over a mountain in a dust storm. I was very frightened, especially since there had been no storm warning. I came down from the mountain to a little town and spent the night in a motel.

In the morning, I saw there had been a blizzard during the night. But I couldn't stay out in no man's land in a motel; I had to go on, get out on the highway in the car. And suddenly, blinded on the highway by snow swirling in front of my eyes, there was another car; it was right in front of me and it was upon me and there was a crash. A sliding. My car was hurled along the ice, out of control, then landed in a ditch, overturned and spun.

I was thinking, *I'm going to die. I don't want to die, but I can't help dying now; it's out of my hands. What a dirty trick to die now. I hope it will be quick.* Then the crash and the whirl and the spin ceased.

There was total silence in the ice and snow and a feeling for feeling – for one's leg, one's face, a tentative opening of one's eyes. *Am I alive, am I here, am I whole?*

2

In September, 1967, I joined around forty other Americans to meet with delegations of North and South Vietnamese in Bratislava, Czechoslovakia, for a conference on peace and the war.

A Vietnamese and I were discussing, over a meal, some of the ambiguities posed by words. He wrote on a paper napkin the word 'thu,' which has in his language *five different meanings*, each dependent on markings. By itself, without any markings, 'thu' means 'autumn'. However, if one places a period beneath the letter *u* in the word, it means 'to benefit by'. Given other markings, it can mean 'enemy', 'pleasure' and 'grasp' – hold in one's arm *or* hold in one's hand.

Then I realized how complex were the words which many people, both in Vietnam and America, would have used to describe *us* at the conferences: 'Communists', 'Vietcong' and 'American imperialists'.

But, first, we were people. There seems to be a universal usage of words which is designed to keep people from knowing each other.

3 *I Often Wonder Where in Hell*

do I belong – in the northern Minnesota woods? the Colorado mountains? the hills and ranchlands? I like them all and get some feeling of affinity with all of them, but always there is the wonder . . . is this really the place? I can't generate the old enthusiasm for new places, new things, new people that I could once. I guess this is a part of changing values. This sounds more depressing than it is intended to be. It's not so much mental depression as a curiosity about one's feelings.

Letter from a middle-aged newspaperman

4

In the early sixties, after I had written some plays, I also appeared in productions of them in coffeehouse theatres in Detroit, in community centres in rural Mississippi and Alabama before black audiences which had often never seen a play or ever been inside a theatre, on Ivy League campuses, and in the National Cathedral in Washington, D.C.

Each audience – even on successive nights in the same theatre – was different. A laugh would not emerge at all where, the night before, the rafters had shaken with laughter. But, without warning, a laugh would suddenly crop up at a place where a laugh was *impossible* before. So I would ask myself – what did the laugh mean, what precisely was the audience expressing?

And then I discovered how useful laughter can be as a means of focusing soberly on a serious question. Laughter is a common acknowledgement of the absurd. An experience of the absurd, shared openly by a vulnerable audience, permits a storyteller to work in a dimension of truth which would otherwise have remained hidden. Now the chips are down. Now people are compelled to focus together – even if only for a moment – on a single shared experience.

5 *His Suicide Shocked A Large Number of People*

He was a gentle, scholarly man. When he spoke, it was with a faintly discernible hesitation which caused him to express himself laboriously and with long pauses. He was an incredibly kind man. In his rooms at the university he would invite for lunch small groups of students who felt alienated from life there.

In his last letter to me, written only four days before his suicide, he said: 'I was away in Asia last summer. I was invited to be examiner in philosophy in the University of Hong Kong; and I combined this with visits to colleges, universities and Christian university teachers' groups in Japan and India. I had a term's leave from Oxford, and was away four and a half months altogether. It was most enjoyable and I felt it very worth while. Now I am back in Oxford again, feeling the Oxford school of philosophy moving further and further away from me, and finding myself very inadequate in guiding my pupils to cope with it. My next task must be to equip myself a little better for this purpose. I am trying to keep this summer vacation as free as possible for this re-educational task.'

I believe he took his life because the academic community

was a cold, airless ghetto within which, at a certain moment, he had needed a strong, unsentimental support it could not give.

Why not?

6 *Love*

I always thought that was something on a beach or done in some motel, but it's not that at all. It's being human and CARING, goddamnit! Jesus was a man. Not a pure, angelic creature with pale-blue know-it-all eyes and a goldilocks hair-cut. You couldn't tell if he was Negro or white or Jewish or whatever. He was a rugged man who roamed the desert and in anger upset the money-lenders' tables in the temple. Perhaps even after getting all hepped up after one of his sermons he grabbed some willing dame and screwed the daylights out of her. And his gospel was love, not necessarily understanding but just love and caring. Jesus was a man, the son of man, and therefore, if you want to look at it that way, the son of that abstract 'God' who created the universe.

I was so occupied, good old Sartre, in the absurdity of life that I forgot man has within him the ability to make it not absurd; not through the hypocrisy which has been preached to me all my life, 'the Big Shit,' but through himself, his abilities and capacity for honesty.

I see now man's greatest virtue is not his intellectual poten-tial, but his social instinct and the hardest of all virtues to culti-vate: his ability to love.

Letter from a woman college student

7 *Winter Day*

Snow is falling. I heard its silence as soon as I woke up, before I looked out of my window.

I imagine that I am in Moscow. It is 1700. Two cossacks

appear on the street, wearing long coats and fur hats. It is 1350, and I am in Paris. I am cold, very, very cold, standing outside a great stone cathedral. It is 1850, London, and now a carriage rumbles down the street.

I must get up. I shall walk through this snow, crunching underfoot, moving from one warm room to another.

I want instead to stay in Moscow, in Paris, in London. I want to live out *those* plots. But will I be the same? Will I believe deeply in the divine right of kings and know how to prepare a superb roast? Will I care for poetry, city planning, discussions of metaphysics, and accept torture as one of the facts of life?

I must get up.

8

Tennessee Williams' *Cat on a Hot Tin Roof* was playing on Broadway. Having recently been ordained a priest, I was in New York completing graduate studies. I wanted to see the play, and friends with show-business connections gave me a ticket worth its weight in gold.

In my black clerical suit and spanking white collar (I was then just getting used to both), I was ushered to the sixth row, centre. It was a matinée, attended almost exclusively by suburban matrons – and me. As the explosive lines flew, reaching a great climax in the outburst at the second-act curtain, the ladies from the suburbs were about to expire from embarrassment – this entirely attributable to the benign presence in their midst of an earnest young priest busily becoming adjusted to wearing clerical garb out in the world. The young priest wanted to turn, at the wave of a magic wand, into a cat, a hot tin roof, or just about anything or anybody else. But he remained himself and lived to tell the tale. Don't we always?

contains as many ambiguities within it as, say, reciting the Nicene Creed, singing 'The Star Spangled Banner' or uttering the words 'I love you.'

10

Hi, Sandy
   (Smile for Ed and Jean, Sandy. You smiled so nicely
   before. Can you wave and say hi?)
What will you become when you grow up, Sandy?
Good girl, Sandy
   (Show Ed and Jean how you can walk, Sandy. That's
   right. Can you walk all the way over here? Come on . . .)
What will you feel when you fall in love, Sandy?

So long, Sandy
   (Oh, Sandy, you've been so mean today. I'm going to
   put you in your crib unless you behave. Now sit up and
   eat your supper. Stop crying, Sandy. Smile. Smile, Sandy)
Will we leave you a world to grow up in, Sandy?

11

To a member of the first parish which I served as a priest:
   I think we tossed off traditional terms too glibly, without
looking for real meanings. For example: We often used the
word 'fellowship' and meant a picnic-basket church social
instead of suffering with, or for, other people. We said 'love'
and meant sending food to a very poor family, but not making
a real sacrifice to change actual conditions causing the poverty.
We said 'success' and meant comfort and things money can
buy, but not, like St. Peter, hanging upside down on a cross
because of a commitment which would not be betrayed. We

spoke of 'sin' and gave it sexual overtones, yet gave little thought to the sin of living complacently with social injustices.

One hour on one day a week. That was our great concept of the meaning of the church. Oh, yes, we had occasional bazaars, suppers and rummage sales. *Not* ecumenically. We operated these things in the spirit of a closed corporation. Once we had too much dissension over a bazaar, and, as a result, the women's organization in the church split into warring factions!

Politics? Race? Economic questions? Social problems? The arts? *No!* Our church was interested only in 'religion'. All of us shared in the guilt of perpetuating the religious ghetto and of keeping our church out of the mainstream of life outside its walls. At the same time, we decorated the altar and made the sanctuary as splendid as possible. In one way or another, all of us seemed to share in an unspoken resolution to love within the liturgy but to withhold love outside the liturgy, from one another and certainly from our closest neighbours up and down the streets.

12

I never saw the gas chamber because I didn't want to see it, but I did see smoke rising from the crematoria chimneys twenty-four hours a day and the scarlet glow over them at night, and day and night I smelled the acrid fumes of burning human flesh and bones. I did not see the little white house in a birchwood to which were driven crowds of people just off trains which had brought them from every corner of Europe. There were days when the smoke covered the entire heavens like a thick shroud as if to make people forget there had ever been a sky, as if the murderers had no more to fear and those to be murdered could understand finally that there was no hope left anywhere.

I was not present at the selection in the hospital when several hundred French girls were taken away. When the horrible

24

shouts of '*Lagersperre*!' rang out, and we heard the sound of trucks stopping in the hospital area, our hearts almost stopped beating and we huddled close to the walls of our barracks. We heard nothing. But when the engines started again and the trucks drove off, their headlights blazing in the dark, carrying these French women to their deaths, the sound of the 'Marseillaise' rang out in the stillness of the night. I shall never forget that. The song grew, stronger and more powerful, filling every corner of the darkness and tearing at our hearts as we stood there frozen with fear and horror. It was a herald of some terrible day of wrath and it reached up into the perpetual scarlet glow that never faded from the night sky.

I did see Greek women 'going to the gas'. They had been brought to Auschwitz only weeks before, slender, black-eyed Salomes, homesick for their sunny land and huddled together against the sleet and cold of the northern October. They sang a sentimental song called 'Mama,' whose melody made one weep. In a few weeks Auschwitz had withered those exotic flowers, their fiery eyes had become dull in sunken sockets, empty and dead. Emaciated, dirty, repulsive, those Greek women could barely drag themselves around. Once so shapely, they now had legs like sticks and their breasts hung like bags. Their complexions, made velvet smooth by the southern sun, were now covered with horrible abscesses, vermin bites, and the marks of scabies incessantly scratched. They stank of gangrene, dysentery, unwashed sweat, and wretchedness.

When they went to their deaths they sang the 'Hatikvah', that song of undying hope, the song of an old people which has always carried the vision of Zion in its heart. Since then, every time I hear 'Hatikvah' I always see them, the dregs of human misery, and I know that through mankind flows a stream of eternity greater and more powerful than individual deaths.

I cannot describe even a fraction of the horror that was Auschwitz, but what I did see was enough to make me lose

for ever the notion that man was created in the likeness of God.
From "Lena's Story," in 'The Holocast Kingdom' by Alexander Donat.

13 *Riccardo:*

And then – then we go home?
Confess – what should we confess?
That we have used the name of God in vain!
And sit down to some journal, to read about
the excavations in St. Peter's?
And then on Sunday we ring the bells
and celebrate our Mass – so filled with sacred thoughts,
that nothing, surely, tempts us to consider
those who at that very moment in Auschwitz
are being driven naked into the gas.

From 'The Deputy' by Rolf Hochhuth

14

This is the jet set, in miniature, but solid gold.

The incredible importance of some persons in the room momentarily stuns me. This represents a kind of *total* power in connections and untold wealth.

Cool. Everybody seems secure. After all, there are no climbers, no interlopers; this is 'family' by intent. Drinks move quickly. A buffet, to be served by a large number of servants standing around a table, waits. On *this* wall hangs an El Greco, on *that* a Van Gogh.

The women are almost primitively dressed. (It would be gauche to 'dress' in the 'family'.) The men are a bit more formal. The conversation has many levels, and *here* I find the insecurities, for no one is really supposed to talk *about* anything but rather just fill (but, damn it, *fill*) a vacuum.

Should we go out on the boat for luncheon tomorrow?

Here is POWER, more than one might find in a great dam. But it is so indolent, so lazy, so ingrown; so permanent.

15 *Masks*

I. I was sitting on the subway coming into New York. Did my face show the strange thing that had happened to me? These other faces, could they tell from my face the reunion I had had, after many years, the reunion linking who I am now with who I was before? These faces, these masks, what had happened to *them* today? Maybe one of them had had a reunion too. But masks are inscrutable. Where are the faces? If we do not have faces and cannot see each other, if this train simply goes on for ever, could this be hell?

II. In museums I see masks which once served the purpose of opening up feeling, expressing emotion, revealing on the surface an inner fear or joy.

Yet, on the street or at a party, over lunch tables and office desks, I see masks which hide feelings and truth.

Sometimes one person needles and jabs at another until a mask falls to the ground, and a human face is seen in its nakedness and beauty. Even a pretty mask is somewhat grotesque and disquieting, so its absence is welcome.

It is absurd when two masks say to one another 'I love you'. It is very touching when two human faces look lovingly upon one another.

16 *Oh, Freedom*

Whadaya want? Freedom.
When? NOW.

17 *The Professor is Moving*

Only a half-dozen people know about it so far.

He's sitting across the living room from me. We're in his faculty house near the small, liberal-arts campus where he has been teaching for five years. His wife is preparing lunch in the kitchen. We're drinking sherry.

'I can't stay,' he says. 'I feel isolated. There's just a very small underground, if you can call it that, of faculty here. My department head is against me. The president has moved against me now. There's no hope here, no hope of doing anything, or changing anything. We've sweated and agonized over this, but what else can we do? I can't fight against these odds. Anyway, I won't be permitted to fight at all. The school wants its dough and the alumni won't put up with any, what it calls, shit. As you know, it's a church-related college, and the board won't have any more to do with race or peace. So we're leaving. What else can we do?'

18 *A Prayer*

I just failed completely, Jesus. I can hardly talk to you at all, or anybody.

I didn't do this very important thing I should, and could, have done.

They were down there waiting for me to do my part and I didn't show. I just sat here and let the time go by. I didn't move, and pretty soon the hour had passed, and so had my chance to be with them when they needed me.

Jolt me out of this lethargy, Jesus. Give me a will to act again. Shock me out of this selfishness so I can go where people really are, and where you want me to be with them and you.

19 *How Does the Frantically Busy Housewife*

(Girl Scout leader, church worker, part-time office worker, tired-out wife and mother, chauffeuse, cook, dressmaker, hostess, etc., etc.) actually know what God's will is for her? And how does she combine all the demands on her time and energy from God and Christ and from her family and community and not LOSE HER MIND?

Letter from a housewife

20

I mean – people don't intend it, but sometimes they end up by not communicating with each other any more. I know an actual case where a couple had never had an even rudimentary talk together. There had never been a discussion, for example, about sexual need. She wasn't really turning him on, and he certainly wasn't meeting her needs, and suddenly she was mad when he had been out with every woman between Des Moines, Iowa, and Bangor, Maine. It was only after that, that they sat down and began trying to talk for the first time. It's not relevant whether that couple made it or not, but this is an example; you take two people who are thrown into very separate worlds – the man working outside all day, the woman working in the home – and then they meet in the evening. I want to know, what is going to be the nature of the meeting?

The author, during a dialogue with James Coburn, the actor

21

Who am I?
Nobody (I feel), now.
I am nobody (is it not so? surely it is so) when I am lonely. I am nobody when I care so desperately, yet do not know for what I care.
I am nobody when I and everything seems to be lost. What does it matter? I want to run away (I am nobody) and to be free and to do nothing (everything) and to be somebody.

29

I want to be me . . . but who (what) am I? I am white (am I not black?) I am American (am I not European?) I am young (oh, God, I feel so old! or do I feel just nothing? ought I not to, if I am nobody?).

Do I know what life is . . . what love is? (Am I somebody?) Have I been loved . . . have I loved? (Am I somebody?) Have I made a mark at all: on a heart, on another life, on the earth, on a piece of paper, on a piece of wood? (Am I somebody?)

Yes! Yes, I have! There *is* a heart . . . There *is* a piece of paper . . . There *is* a piece of wood . . .

Where is the heart? *Where* is the piece of paper? *Where* is the piece of wood? Where is the mark? What is the mark?

I can show you. (No, I can't show you.) You must believe me. There *is* a heart. There *is* a piece of paper. There *is* a piece of wood. Please, you must believe me.

From 'If I Go Down to Hell' by the author

22

Beginnings are awkward, time-consuming, interesting, and lead inevitably toward involvements.

Endings are wise, functional and sad.

23 *At The Flicks:* The Red Desert

She cries, more to herself than to anyone else: 'Why do I always need other people?'

24 *Mirror, Mirror on the Wall:*

What's the matter with you this morning?

25

It is a nonverbal afternoon, a decidedly nonverbal situation, and all of us are struck virtually numb by complex nonverbal feelings amid a pervasive, shared nonverbal mood.

So why is someone making small talk?

26 *My Father Acts Like,*

and sometimes even goes as far as to tell me, he doesn't trust me. How come?

Letter from a teen-age girl

27

Shortly after I had been ordained an Episcopal priest, I was assigned to conduct services one Sunday morning in a small neighbourhood parish. Just as the procession down the centre aisle was about to start, a lady approached me to ask a pressing question. 'What was Jesus's religion?' The organist had already begun the processional hymn. I had no time for fancy explanations, just bare facts. 'He was a Jew,' I replied.

'Oh, then my husband was right,' the woman countered. 'We were arguing about it last night. He told me Jesus was a Jew, but I had always thought he was Lutheran.'

28 *He Isn't Married*

He doesn't believe in the institution called marriage. It would interfere with his relationships. Sex would not be so good any more, he believes, because suddenly there would be moralizing, and convention.

A different chick every night, no strings, fun, laughs, no hang-ups. Who wants to get involved? Who wants to get hurt? He knows he doesn't.

He considers himself a master of the art of loving and is proud of his credentials. He likes to say 'I love you', but can't stand to hear the words. 'Damn it,' he tells a startled woman, 'leave love out of it.'

What is he looking forward to? 'Tomorrow night,' he says with a smile. He seems invulnerable, and then suddenly a girl he has been dating off and on asks him whether he would like to be a father. He has a moment's anger: How could she be so stupid and how does she know it's his and why doesn't she take care of it without him?

But then he tries the words 'my son' under his breath, and looks at the girl. Maybe she's only kidding.

29 *I Decided to Try Them*

Not everything, but the right ones. Ad men would henceforth be my prophets. They talked about such pleasant things, always on the bright side – except for the day when the postman would leave the bills. But, the ad men said, pay by instalments.

I bought the right car, the right gin, the right suits, the right TV set, the right chocolates, the right deodorant, the right coffee, the right suppositories and the right life insurance.

I switched to the right cigarette, the right newspaper, the right vermouth, the right church, the right suntan ointment, the right undergarment, the right news magazine and the right air-line.

And what did I find? Milk and honey! My image and I are now exact. I'm no longer me, I'm *it*.

MARCH

1 *I Am in the Doctor's Office*

It's so damned frightening. I've got to have help. I'm in such pain I honestly can't stand much more of it, but, on an impulse, I'd run out of the door. *Now*.

Now it's too late. A nurse has spoken to me. I look at the pile of old magazines – they're awful; I've read them all. The air is antiseptic, stale, dry. Three other people are waiting in the office, and we studiously avoid meeting one another's eyes. This becomes embarrassing when one woman, reading something, keeps chuckling out loud; her leg is in a plaster cast which is marked by several autographs (from children? neighbours? office associates?).

It seems as if I've been here for an hour. My throat is very dry. I couldn't be more uneasy if I were on a bed of nails. (Why is the office furniture so uncomfortable?) I look at my watch; I've been waiting twelve minutes.

A door opens. Does it lead to a holy of holies? Surely, there are great mysteries behind the door – hard questions and maybe hard answers. Someone's name is being called. I continue to wait, now thumbing through the pages of a magazine I read a month ago and disliked just as much then as I do now. What mysteries will I find when the door opens for me?

2 *I'm Getting a Whole Bunch of New Ideas*

about this world, and everything is just swirling about in my head. Right now I feel so small and insignificant, and ignorant, and I mean, what can *I* do in this world? Men are killed every day, by hundreds, for what they feel and believe, and some are being denied the right to feel and believe. What is right, are they all wrong, what's the *real* truth? Probably typical freshman-in-college ideas, about having a 'cause' and all, but it really bugs me, it bothers me. And about God. I don't know. I haven't been to church since I've been in college. My mother doesn't know; you know, I just remembered that she once said to me that the least I could do for her is to go to church on Sunday with her, 'cause I never do anything else for her. And I feel ashamed now, I can feel a lump rising in my throat. I feel sorry for her, I hope I never have a daughter like I have been. Our trouble was that we never communicated. I am afraid to talk to her because then I feel that she'll know something about me that I don't want her to know, and then I feel ashamed that she knows it. It's a sad situation. I just can't express my love to her, and I know she loves me. Hey, thanks for listening to all this.

Letter from a woman college freshman

3 Isn't It Blasphemous to Say

you take Jesus Christ with you into a homosexual bar?

4

It was early Saturday morning at Union Station . . . before the train left Washington, D.C. for the New York peace march.

The crowd of 1100 (the 300 overflow had gone on buses rented at the last minute) epitomized that old-saw tag 'cross-section': about 40 per cent Negro; lots of high school students; a sprinkling of beards and sandals; a surprising number of middle-aged couples, looking a little as if they were off to visit a daughter at a college they had never heard of . . . And scattered through the crowded aisles with their very special expression of flat-heeled middle-class zeal were smiling hardworking members of the Women's Strike for Peace, responsible for youth groups for the entire organization . . .

The New York arrival was incredibly orderly . . . It was 4 P.M. before we were on Central Park South. It grew colder, and the pauses for traffic lights seemed to be longer and longer. . . . Suddenly we were abreast of the Plaza Hotel with red-coated waiters peering from windows. Occasionally a sympathetic tenant opened a window and clapped. Long-haired girls in party dresses looking like the cover of 'Vogue for Children' and apparently at a party on the second floor, held up paper napkins on which they had drawn peace symbols with black Magic Markers. . . .

And finally, we were at Forty-seventh Street. The U.N. Plaza was filled and we could not edge close enough to see the familiar tall façade. 'The speeches are all over,' said a man with a transistor radio. The crowd around us started to disperse immediately, many retracing their steps.

'What no one understands,' my friend said, 'is that there is a mystique that pervades things like this. Somehow you feel the re-establishment of human dignity.'

From an account of the New York peace march by Jenny Moore

5

If any man ever dared to translate all that is in his heart, to put down what is really his experience, what is truly his truth, I think then the world would go to smash, that it would be blown to smithereens and no god, no accident, no will could ever again assemble the pieces, the atoms, the indestructible elements that have gone to make up the world.

From 'Tropic of Cancer' by Henry Miller

6 *Organized Religion*

is the glue in the spit of the Establishment.

7

I have always been fond of the response a student made to a policeman who, upon entering a raucous college beer joint near a campus where I served as chaplain, was confused to find me sitting around midnight at a table and talking with a group of students.

'What's he doing here?' the policeman asked the student somewhat angrily.

'Well, sir,' the student replied, 'I think he's saying goodnight to his parish.'

8 *Fun*

Leisure is downright kooky, isn't it? I mean, in my own case, if you put me under a beach umbrella and say 'relax,' I freeze. But I can downright enjoy some kinds of hard work.

It's leisure when I can relax and like what I'm doing, become engrossed in the work and forget time schedules and pressures. But it's fun when what I'm doing (perhaps even some kind of FUN) is like pulling teeth. I'm sweating hard over it, hate it, and wish a bell would ring somewhere to spring me loose.

Freedom, then, seems to be closely related to leisure. Freedom inside.

It might help a lot if society, especially airline public-relations folk and chic magazines (involved in a wild FUN fetish, while remaining unknowing slaves to the Protestant-Ethic-hangover), could relax.

9 *A Teen-Age Boy*

comments about sex: 'I like many girls. The majority of them are "champions". The only problem is that I don't want to go with them, but would like to make fun with them, especially sexwise. What should I do? I have a pamphlet on sex relations called *To Thread a Needle* which actually goes into detail about how to perform the love act; and I would like to know if there is anything you could do to have sex information given to young people so that they will know more about how to get more out of life.'

10

Churchwoman: I don't want the world to come into the church.

And I don't want the church to get involved in the world. I want to keep them separate, completely separate, so that once a week on Sunday mornings I can walk outside the world – oh, I get sick and tired of it – and walk into the church building which is a world all by itself, untarnished by the sadness and cruelty of the world outside. I long for this. I wait for this all week. It's like heaven to escape out of the world into the refreshing, cool beauty of the church building, with its choir and its colours and its familiarity. I know heaven will be like this. Alone, in a church congregation, singing, with beautiful flowers on an altar, and God instructing us how to live comfortably and serenely for another week.

From an unpublished play, 'The Community', by the author

11 *You Feel About Such Handsome and Charming Men*

that life has been unkind to them in treating them kindly. I guess part of the inner tragedy of the whole film colony is this being swaddled in the world's image of its own life. Then, when the cellophane is harshly torn away, they look at their spiritual destitution and recognize their defencelessness in the presence of man. Also their need of an incarnate Christ who is willing to become an actor for the sake of actors. If only

37

they knew that He has lived that death with them already, and worn the mask of their flesh.

Letter from a theologian who had just visited Hollywood for the first time

12 *Black, We All Know*

is the colour of night, sin, evil and death. And white is the colour of light, purity, holiness and resurrection after death. Easter lilies are white (virgins must be too) and Christ is always pictured in a white robe that matches his white face. But since his face wasn't white – he was a deeply-tanned Semite – maybe his robe wasn't either. So maybe everything else that is supposed to be pure and holy doesn't have to be white. Would it be grey? *Could it be black?* Could the awful black pit be pure and holy? And could a white heart be a sepulchre of death?

13 *Travel Note*

Being an airline employee would be as awful as hiring oneself out to a movie studio: a terrible, gnawing drabness, over and over and over again, under a fake illusion of glamour.

14

A terrible thought, but true. . . . I suspect that if I knew that when we die, it's over, there's nothing and *that's it,* I really believe I'd be living a better life now, a fuller life with the juice wrung out of every waking moment. I'm using eternity, or heaven *or* reincarnation (which is a nice thought, you must admit) as a convenient cop-out for being lazy and uncreative, and stagnant right *now*. Like, if there's more to come, why worry too much about it now?

Letter from a college student

15 *Karl Marx and Sigmund Freud*

should be taught in Sunday School.

16

Paint is peeling off the walls in the run-down diner in a city slum.

Unemployed men sit silently at the counter sipping coffee. The wooden door is rotting. The chairs are wobbly. It is cold, inside and out.

The jukebox is playing 'I Wish You Love.'

17 *A Prayer*

I lied, Jesus. I wanted to lie and I did.

I know it didn't do me any good. In fact, I never thought it would. I just decided to tell the lie.

In a funny way I think I just wanted to raise some hell with things, you know? I was getting bored and something had to give around here. So I gave.

Now what am I supposed to do? Things seem to be in a real bind, Jesus, because it was a big lie. Everybody's in a stew about it. You'd think I committed a murder or something, Lord.

You know I didn't mean it that way. Do I have to straighten things out, Jesus, by saying I lied? Lord, give me some time to think about this, will you? I wish everybody else could understand that I feel damned sorry about this, and ashamed.

18 *At the Flicks:* Murder in the Cathedral

Make love, not war.

19

'Love! Love!' he said. 'Not war, not force! Even prayer, Brother Bernard, is not enough; good works are needed too. It is difficult and dangerous to live among men, but necessary. To withdraw into the wilderness and pray is too easy, too convenient. Prayer is slow in producing its miracles; works are faster, surer, more difficult. Wherever you find men, you will also find suffering, illness, and sin. That is where our place is, my brother: with lepers, sinners, with those who are starving. Deep down in the bowels of every man, even the saintliest ascetic, there sleeps a horrible, unclean larva. Lean over and say to this larva: "I love you!" and it will sprout wings and become a butterfly.'

From 'Saint Francis' by Nikos Kazantzakis

20

Our 'Skyraider' was loaded with 750-pound napalm bombs and 500-pound napalm bombs. . . . Our wing load carried 7,500 pounds of high-explosive anti-personnel bombs. We were in the lead plane going in. . . .

As we flew over the target it looked to me very much as the normal village would look: on the edge of a river, sampans and fish nets in the water. It was a peaceful scene. Major Carson put our plane into a steep dive. I could see the napalm bombs dropping from the wings. The big bombs, first. As we peeled back from our dive, I saw an incredibly bright flash of fire as napalm exploded at tree level. The first pass had a one-two effect. The napalm was expected to force the people – fearing the heat and the burning – out into the open. Then the second plane was to move in with heavy fragmentation bombs to hit whoever had rushed out into the open. So our wingman followed us in and dropped his heavy explosives. Mushroom-like clouds drifted into the air. We made a second pass and dropped our remaining 500-pound bombs. Our wingman followed. Then we went in for a third time and raked over the village with our cannon. We came down low, flying very fast, and I could see some of the villagers trying to head away from the burning shore in their sampans. The village was burning fiercely. I will never forget the sight of the fishing nets in flame, covered with burning, jellied gasoline. . . .

There were probably between 1,000 and 1,500 people living in the fishing village we attacked. It is difficult to estimate how many were killed. It is equally difficult to judge if there actually were any Viet Cong in the village, and if so, if any were killed. . . .

From a report by Bernard Fall in 'Ramparts'

21   Saints Aren't Just in Stained-Glass Windows and History Books

Jonathan M. Daniels, the twenty-six-year-old seminarian and civil rights worker who was murdered in Haynesville, Alabama, in 1965, was one of a tiny handful of persons through whom the church – in our own age – becomes actively related to oppressed persons.

Theologically he knew what he was doing, and in a church which seems so often to be on stilts, he was one person who was not afraid of getting involved in the human struggle.

22   'Phony'

is like 'nigger', 'kike' or 'wop': We're inclined to cremate each other, put the ashes in a small box, label it in an inhumanly ugly way, and put it on a shelf.

That way, we don't have to listen to each other.

23 *Absurd*

This divorce between man and his life, the actor and his setting, truly constitutes the feeling of Absurdity.

From 'The Myth of Sisyphus' by Albert Camus

'And I will always stammer, since he spoke,'
One, who had been most eloquent said, stammering.
From 'The Starlight's Intuition Pierced the Twelve' by Delmore Schwartz

I began trying to create an out-of-focus world – a heightened reality better than real, that suggests, rather than tells you. Maybe the fact I'm myopic had something to do with it. When I take off my glasses, especially on rainy nights, I get a far more beautiful view of the world than twenty-twenty people get. I wanted to reproduce this more poetic image that I was privately enjoying.

From 'A Woman Entering a Taxi in the Rain,' by Winthrop Sargeant, in The New Yorker

How do we speak of God without religion . . . How do we speak in a secular fashion of God?

From 'Prisoner for God' by Dietrich Bonhoeffer

24 *We received Seventeen Hate Calls*

one night, in McComb, Mississippi, between midnight and seven A.M. Eight of these were death threats. We were staying in a Freedom House. Students, white and black, living there were working on voter registration among local Negroes.

I was to stand guard outside the house between midnight and three A.M., for the Freedom House had recently been bombed. It was odd, standing alone in the middle of the night, listening for sounds. A dog would bark in the distance. Then I would hear the sound of an approaching car. I would become tense, wondering if *this* car might speed by the house while someone hurled killing sticks of dynamite. . . . The students were sleeping inside. . . . There had already been more than a dozen bombings of Negro homes and churches in that killing summer of 1964. . . .

25

I had visited a state university as a guest speaker. A young Presbyterian chaplain told me afterwards: 'Your visit was a (quote) Success (unquote). So you've given life for another year or two to the religious foundations on the campus. However, that being the case, didn't you really fail?'

He was referring to the increasingly widely shared belief that the church must will to 'die' before it can experience authentic renewal, or a 'resurrection'.

26 *Alvar Aalto*

is a name I'd like to have.

27

You don't have to put up a sign that says 'Dead End' at the end of a road.

You don't need to say 'Jewish rabbi'.

If you are showing a house or apartment that's for rent, and walk into the kitchen, you don't need to say 'This is the kitchen.'

If you are preparing a TV commercial for a commodity that kills insects, you don't need to say 'It kills insects dead.'

28

I'm staying overnight in one of those new luxury hotels

which make the hanging gardens of Babylon look like crab-grass.

It's so *big*. I must time myself carefully, for it requires ten minutes to reach the lobby from my room. I get my exercise simply by walking to and from the lifts.

My bath is a great sunken pool. A biography of the owner of the hotel is placed, alongside a Gideon Bible, in a drawer that also contains an extra blanket and a laundry bag with a draw-string.

The telephone opens up a whole new world for me. I can dial a number for *anything*. Why don't I dial 2 for room service, 3 in order to have my suit pressed, and 4 to scream?

I would love to burn down this monstrous, impersonal, tranquillized, dehumanized pre-morgue, but can't. It's fire-proof.

29 *Good Friday*

A Jewish boy riding along the street on his bicycle on Good Friday afternoon meets a group of school friends. They are dressed up in suits, clean shirts and ties. He is dressed in Levis and a sportshirt, his (and their) usual attire. They are on their way home from a Good Friday church service which consisted of meditations upon the crucifixion of Jesus.

He wheels his bicycle in front of them and prepares to join the group. But his friends are strangely sullen. No one smiles or greets him, and one boy blurts out: ' You killed Christ. You murdered Him.'

30 *Easter (a Prayer)*

Thanks for reminding me again about beauty and joy, Jesus.

I'd forgotten. The permanent ugliness of a lot of things had gotten to me. Joy seemed very remote. I mean, I had got on a kind of treadmill, Lord, in my own life, and everywhere else I looked, I seemed to find pretty much the same thing.

I guess I'd written off mystery. I had everything more or less figured out, and suddenly it seemed indescribably awful and meaningless, Lord. I was thinking, where do I go from here, and, anyhow, why bother?

Now I feel as if a window has opened and I can see through it. I can look outside the lonely, damp tomb I'd been in. Thanks for letting me see colours and patterns and movement again, Jesus.

31 *I Don't Know Where to Go*

to get the ability to love. I am so very afraid of life in its many dimensions. But I want to feel something besides this fear. How do I learn to love? To trust? Over and over I keep hearing the love chapter of Paul. And I am nothing. I know where I am but I don't know how to leave.

Letter from a college student

APRIL

1

Eight Japanese businessmen are on a downtown street in Washington, D.C.

They carry cameras (a sacrament for tourists) and are very, very busy, looking here, poking their heads there, snapping pictures, running to make a traffic light, caught up in their enthusiasm.

I remember December 7, 1941, and how, after the Japanese bombing of Pearl Harbor, there was such bitterness towards everything Japanese. In Washington, cherry blossom trees were uprooted. Detention camps were built for Japanese-American families. Hollywood made some frightening 'B' films about 'the Yellow Menace'. What had been seen as charming and quaint in Japanese manners and customs was now despised and rejected.

Yet today, some twenty-five years after Pearl Harbor, the Japanese businessmen are quite free and accepted. So, mercifully, humanness takes over and people forget the propaganda of wars. However, in the conduct of men's affairs, a war has been presumed to occur every few years. Is this an inescapable part of human life?

The next time, will it be Japanese against Americans (and Americans against Japanese), or Japanese *and* Americans against somebody else?

Must it be either?

2 *Sermon Topic*

printed in ordinary letters on a colourless church bulletin board on a downtown street in a great city:

LIFE IS MYSTERY

3 *The Telephone Rang at 8:25 P.M.*

A man's voice announced: 'You're going to die at eight-thirty.' The man answering the phone was a Negro leader in a small Mississippi town. His caller, a white man, said: 'We want you niggers to get out of the state.' The immediate dilemma of the Negro leader was whether to stay in the house, which might be bombed, or run outside and possibly be shot. He stayed. The hour of 8:30 came and passed without incident. The hate call was repeated at midnight with another death threat. The Negro leader sat up all night.

Then the call came again at 5:00 A.M. 'I'm tired, but I'm still around,' the Negro quietly told his persecutor.

4

While I was still a student in a theological seminary, I was invited one Sunday to preach a guest sermon in a near-by church. Another seminarian and I decided to try an 'innovation' – an attempt to modernize the proceedings, make them more relevant. We had heard about 'dialogue sermons' and felt we should collaborate in giving one. So, on the appointed Sunday morning, shortly after I had begun preaching from the pulpit, a voice from the rear of the small congregation rang out: 'I don't agree with you! You're wrong!' Necks swivelled around so fast that I'm sure some members of the congregation required medical care. And I realized we had failed – failed to 'communicate' because we were making a gimmick out of an essentially fine idea. *Dialogue*, when it's unfettered, is a basic human need. Now I have learned: I'm giving 'sermons'. I try to speak without a plan or notes – in order to be spontaneous and to feel people and respond to them. Afterwards, I build into the 'sermon' itself time for questions and discussion. I feel these 'dialogue sermons' are indeed Christian teach-ins.

5

... dancing to the throb of nigger music, the white man's solace.

From 'Balthazar' by Lawrence Durrell

6

Sign in the Deep South, alongside a winding dirt road:
LAKE FORGETFUL. PRIVATE

7 I Remember a Time

in my life when I hid, with great care, behind high walls I erected between myself and reality. This meant I had to keep human beings on the other side of the wall, too, along with issues and threatening ideas. Then I realized one day that the walls were crumbling, very gradually, very slowly. I knew there would be no Jericho for me, no instantaneous collapse of the walls I had set up, no single giant roar to be followed by clarity and relationship. But even then, as I peered out from behind the crumbling walls, as I had done many times before, for the first time I saw people instead of persons. It seems so important to me now that we see individuals instead of 'suburbanites', 'Negroes', 'liberals', 'WASPs', 'niggers', 'conservatives', 'wops', 'beatniks', 'Jews', 'Birchites', 'kikes', 'Black Nationalists', 'white devils', 'Uncle Toms', 'moderates', 'radicals'. . . . People.

8

Kumbaya
children are starving, Lord
children are crying, Lord
Itta Bena is one of the areas in six Mississippi counties visited

48

recently by a team of doctors. The physicians reported last weekend that children in these areas live outside every legal, medical and social advance the nation had made in this century.

Starvation diets, disease and other conditions in the six counties are not one whit better than the northern part of Kenya, the doctors' report said.

News dispatch by 'United Press International'

At the end of the village a woman lay gasping as blood poured from a wound in her side. Around her were clustered terrified children, wailing and alternately staring in fear at the Marines and turning to clutch the dying woman. . . . The Marines burned down houses from which they believed the Viet Cong had fired. . . .

News dispatch by John Wheeler, Paris 'Herald Tribune'

9 Duet on Deaths

How many deaths must a man die?

A man must die deaths until he dies.

What is the difference between deaths and death?

The deaths of a man are in the spirit, affecting his pride, his isolation, his spiritual murdering of other men, his greed, his exploitation of his brother. The death of a man is in the body as well as in the spirit, and marks his physical annihilation on earth.

How are these deaths related to death itself?

These deaths diminish a man's egoism and multiply his open relationships with other men, as well as increase his awareness of the universe of life surrounding his own personal island. When a man has grown accustomed to dying, which can be translated as living in a broader and deeper sense, he is naturally adjusted to the final act of death itself, which is an act of life.

Why is the act of death an act of life?

Death is inseparable from life. A seed dies, buried deep in the earth, and, after a time, new life is born. Death itself is dynamic, never simply static or isolated from momentum. Its pause, its evident lack of rhythm, is deceptive; for forces of life are gathered and gathering; a body is indeed still and decaying, yet a personality is a great force of incredible diversity and many dimensions. At death, it is something like a symphony which awaits the start of a new movement. In that moment colour may be absent, but not a Hamlet black-and-white. There seems to be silence, but listen: That dead life makes sound which is like the reverberation inside a dead shell torn from the sea. Death is very real, and exists, but not apart from life. Life is very real, and exists, but not apart from death. The finality of each is required of the other.

How are the acts of death related to the acts of life?

Unless a man dies many deaths in the spirit, he cuts himself off from living itself. He comes to misunderstand life, fears other persons, and breaks the very rhythm of living. A man who is most alive knows such deaths intimately. His life, in its openness and continued vulnerability, its absence of hardness or cynicism, is marked by the scars of such deaths. They are the very signs of life in him.

10

Sign in Store Window:

LAMP SHADES
Custom Made
(In memoriam: Ilse Koch)

11 *People Wonder Why He Doesn't Sell Out*

In the first place, he's a bishop, so he's *supposed* to. The 'Ins' assume he will and are, with evident impatience, marking time. The 'Outs' assume he sold out from the beginning, and that it's all an act played for their benefit by the Power Structure (their term, in this instance).

Strangely, he hasn't sold out. Probably he won't.

He's had the same Power Structure training other bishops, and Important Christian Leaders, have had Lunch with Important Leaders at The Club (day after day after day after day). Meetings over a drink, at The Club or at the home of a Very Important Leader, to discuss budget and where it will come from (with a few corollary lessons on How Not to Disturb Big Money). Public dinners, including the mutual-bestowing-of-awards type (such awards alternating with honorary degrees from controlled educational institutions). Membership on The Right Board of Directors – philanthropic, educational, religious and/or business. And pressure, pressure, pressure, pressure, pressure.

So, in his case, what happened?

A number of things, probably. He's not impressed by sham and pomposity, but realizes he must work through these. He's carefully educated in the nature and exercise of power. While he becomes angry about misuse of power and social injustice, he is able to go on loving people, so he remains in communication with them. He's very, very secure within himself, has brushed death (including his own) in the war, is not rapacious about Success, and is driven by circumstances outside himself rather than unmet needs within.

His gospel, for all his sophistication, is essentially a very simple one. Pragmatically, it adds up to: assuming meaning and caring (Faith), striving and developing strategies to improve society (Hope), and service (Love).

12 Two Cars at Night on a Highway

One car in the distance, just two lights, like two very small bright eyes on the horizon, coming closer, closer, now very close, now they are here, now they have passed, now there is blackness. . . . We will never know each other.

13 *I Am Always Terrified*

when anyone talks about starting a 'new' religion. I can't help thinking that we'll have to go through the Inquisition and the Crusades again. For God's sake, let's try instead to work with what we've *got*. It cost us a few centuries, bloodshed, mistakes, an arrogant lack of charity, *and*, yes, love. Let's make love now, not ' new' religions!

14 *A Prayer*

The people are dancing, Jesus.

The music is loud, so loud it seems to shut out everything else. The people are not dancing in a stylized way. They're expressing a strong desire for freedom and individuality.

Look at that young girl dancing, Jesus. She is moving easily to the rhythm and seems not to have a nerve in her body. And the heavy, middle-aged man – over there, in his shirtsleeves – is unselfconscious and having a good time.

Jesus, how did Christianity ever get mixed up with puritanism and a sense of shame about honest pleasure? Help us to celebrate life with you and the others you have placed us with, Lord.

15

I suspect, with my logical side, that the thing with Jesus and myth and history is a problem in semantics, a problem in the 'way' I'm looking at the New Testament. But I feel that if the stories about resurrection of the dead and miracles are not true (historically) that something is missing, that perhaps Jesus doesn't deserve adoration, but only respect as a 'good guy'. But then I become one of those who needs signs in order to believe. And I get hopelessly caught in a web of not knowing what to think. And, as a result, I can't feel.

What does it mean to take up 'my cross' and follow Jesus? What did Jesus mean when he said that he who loses his life for his (Jesus's) sake shall find it? (It reeks of things Eastern.) And what would Jesus think of what we have done to him, if he came back today and saw newspaper ads about Easter clothes, and looked into churches, and walked through a seminary?

Letter from a college student

16

Mentally, I checked out of here three hours ago. I just turned off. I am looking at it as a *past* event. (I have even packed my suitcase, said some goodbyes without labelling them, and gone out of my way to let some persons know I was not reacting against them, but rather simply against ideological 'positions'.)

Yet I am still here, and will be for another day.

At the outset of this conference, I assumed everybody cared about it with a kind of terrible intensity. So I suppose I could not support my own, isolated hurt when I discovered how wrong I was.

The point of the conference has snapped loose from its tight coil and, dizzyingly, one looks in vain for the original vision of it which was – yes – a momentarily shared experience. Individual interests overtook group conviction before I was aware this was happening.

Too, a set of group cliques has shattered all pretensions about shared openness. Even sensitive awareness of one another – my God, was that only an illusion too? – has given way to coldly functional mechanics.

I fantasize that it is all a past event. It is not. It is happening.

17 *Sunday Morning at 11 O'clock:*

still the most segregated single hour in American society.

18

About a week later, the same guard asked me to move a three-hundred-pound log. I told him I wouldn't. He started to hit me with a big stick he picked up off the ground. He hit me fifteen or twenty times. I grabbed the stick out of his hand and threw it away, and said that if he ever hit me again, 'me and him was going to have it'. He pulled out his gun and started backing up and shaking and saying: 'Nigger, I ought to kill you.' Then he put me in a truck and took me back to the county farm, and took me to the superintendent and told the superintendent that I had hit him. Then they put me in a car and brought me back to the county jail and threw me in solitary.

I was in solitary for 36 hours. The cell was 9 × 12, a 'sweat-box'. I was naked. The cell was a big steel vault in the ground, with no windows. They turned on heated air into the vault, and left it on all the time I was in the cell. Then they came back and took me back to the county farm. They started asking me questions such as, whether I was ready to 'act right'. I said, 'If somebody treat me right.' They said that everything would be okay.

Then they put me back on the same road gang. After about one week, the guard . . . pulled out a long hosepipe again and started to beat me one day without provocation. He struck me about ten or fifteen times. I asked him why he had done that. He said: 'you one of them smart-ass niggers. I don't like your ass.' He took me back again to the county jail. I was put in a cell for about four days until I was released.

. . . I am a resident of Jackson, Negro, 22 years of age.

Signed: Jesse Harris
From 'Mississippi Black Paper'

19 Guerrilla Theology:

How many seminaries are teaching it?

20

Jesus's rage did not abate. 'I say one thing, you write another, and those who read you understand still something else! I say: Cross, death, Kingdom of Heaven, God . . . and what do you understand? Each of us attaches his own sufferings, interests and desires to each of these sacred words, and My words disappear, My soul is lost. I can't stand it any longer!'

He rose, suffocating. Suddenly he felt his mind and heart being filled with sand.

The disciples cowered. It was as though the Rabbi still held the ox-goad and pricked them as though they were sluggish oxen who refused to move. The world was a cart to which they were yoked; Jesus goaded them on, and they shifted under the yoke, but did not budge. Looking at them Jesus felt drained of all his strength.

The road from earth to heaven was a long one and there they were motionless.

From 'The Last Temptation of Christ' by Nikos Kazantzakis

21 The Unloved

It's a church located in the heart of a great city. Life goes on at a furious pace around it. People hurry along the streets outside it. In the neighbourhood there is real poverty, human need of every imaginable kind, success and failure, buying and selling, speaking and listening, despair and hope.

But the church is an alien island amid life. It bars its doors against the people outside, yet few seek to enter it, except perhaps to make love in an empty pew or seek a moment's rest inside that vast, silent cavern of stone.

Expensive vestments of velvets and silks are locked in closets in the back of the church. A jewelled chalice, kept on a shelf, is used only on rare festivals. The church members drive into the neighbourhood only once a week, to worship and flee. They are building a church nearer their new houses in a middle-class, monochromatic, restricted neighbourhood.

It disturbs them that government agencies have taken over traditional charitable tasks of working with the poor and needy. Aside from distributing food baskets a couple of times a year (a woman in a house down the street was quite rude not long ago about *that*), they want nothing to do with the old neighbourhood. Isn't the church a place for *worship*? Well, they say, then let it attend to its business.

Now it is evening. The old church is gloomy, deserted, filled with strange sounds and shadows. It is ugly, unloved, and will be torn down soon to make room for a new parking lot.

22

I worked in Hollywood during the early days of television. One couldn't specialize then and as a result, I produced shows, wrote scripts, and even appeared in one series where I interviewed celebrity guests.

On one show, candidates for Miss Firecracker were the guests. Miss Firecracker was to be honoured in a giant fireworks show in Los Angeles. These were the early days of TV, remember, when lessons could be learned only by experience: one's own. And, everybody was still experimenting with answers to such basic problems as how to photograph colours. The candidates for Miss Firecracker wore bathing suits in a variety of colours on the TV show.

However, several suits *photographed* as flesh colour. Well, the studio switchboard lit up like a Christmas decoration. Not only the decency zealots were calling that night, but also some viewers to express their approval in highly questionable language. The young switchboard operator was bent over the popping lights, crying.

In those faraway pioneer days of TV, we had learned something new. (Remember *us* when you look at colour television.)

23 Sacred Cows

must be absolutely shocked to find themselves in the midst of a blood bath.

24 Celebrity

By the time you read this it will be old news that the fabulous Marilyn Monroe has arrived in London. But to me right now it is new news, the newsiest of news, and, it would seem, the biggest news in years. Whatever you may have read about the fantastic welcome 'The Shape' received when she arrived here is true. Simply because it would be quite impossible to exaggerate the impact the 'calendar blonde' made on this country, its people, and its newspapers. This is really a case of an event that beggars description.

Milton Deane, in 'The Hollywood Reporter'

I had everything but love.

Diana Barrymore, in 'Look'

She came into my office looking like a dream in a skin-tight, beige-rose princess gown embroidered in tiny pearls. She was sporting a charm bracelet and earrings, gifts of husband Ray Anthony, and a pearl anklet. Mamie's baby was but six weeks old; she had just seen her latest picture, 'Star in the Dust'. Mamie was enthusiastic about her son Perry: 'He has dark hair and eyes like Ray.' But the gist of her conversation that day was that blonde, busty and Beautiful Mamie wanted out of her contract.

Hedda Hopper, in an interview with actress Mamie Van Doren, in the Los Angeles 'Times'

Reach opinion leaders and you reach the masses.

Dr Paul Lazarsfeld, in 'Printers' Ink'

I shall never forget the day I toiled along the Via Dolorosa with the huge symbol that has carried the message of mercy through the ages. Great crowds stood for hours in the blazing sun and numbers lined the walls and covered the roofs of houses. The crowds around my carriage were so dense that police were told to keep the people back. When I left the carriage to take up my position in the scene a way was made for me with no word said. Women stepped forward and kissed my robe.

From a memoir by R. Henderson Bland, who portrayed Christ iu the film 'From the Manger to the Cross' (1912)

25

In a delta province there is a woman who has both arms burned off by napalm and her eyelids so badly burned that she cannot close them. When it is time for her to sleep her family puts a blanket over her head. The woman had two of her children killed in the air strike which maimed her last April and she saw five other children die. She was quite dispassionate when she told an American 'more children were killed because the children do not have so much experience and do not know how to lie down behind the paddy dikes'.

From 'Evergreen Review'

26 *Spring Day*

A leaf which had been captured inside ice is now part of a running stream which had been frozen.

Can *I* strike out for freedom?

27

A big fly has got into my room. My first impulse was to kill him.

But why?

I think now he is trying to make friends with me. On his terms, of course.

How can I find out what they are?

28 *At the Flicks:* Bonnie and Clyde

From Indian massacres to Vietnam, and from the Boston Tea Party to Newark in the summer of 1967, America has been a violent country, man.

29

It is not a time for reflection, but for evocation. The responsibility of the intellectual is the same as that of the street organizer, the draft resister, the Digger: to talk *to* people, not *about* them. The important literature now is the underground press, the speeches of Malcolm, the works of Fanon, the songs of the Rolling Stones and Aretha Franklin.

From 'Soul Power' by Andrew Kopkind

30 *Time*

I feel my life is ebbing away and I don't know what to do about it. I can't seem to get control of myself right now. I make resolutions, one after another (I *mean* this one, damn it), but can't keep them. I'm still in a funk, desperate, restless, tired, uncommunicable.

I guess I realize my life *is* ebbing away. It's an hour later than it was, or a day. I know I have that much less time. I am, and am not, at the mercy of time. It plagues me, even when I understand best how time does not limit or imprison me.

Life is out there, *there*, on the street where the sun is shining. The air is stirring against people's legs, arms and faces. And life is *here*. If I were to open a window, could *there* become *here*, and *here* become *there*?

I ask myself: If I were to die today – and had just four hours' notice – what would I really want to do?

I would really want to go from *here* to *there*. I would want to celebrate life by sharing it.

I can do this now.

MAY

1 *The Mozart Sonata*

in B-flat major for violin and piano is playing. Except for the record, the room is silent.

I am in a moment of solitude. The sun and clouds through the high windows are making stark, fluid reflections on the white wall. An immense tree through the window seems my nearest companion; it is so much older than I, and will outlive me. (Is he wise? I am not.)

What am I to do with this solitude? I could let it project me out of myself or else I could sink deep into myself. But what, or who, is myself? The journey into self, if I choose that way, is like Mongolian land: remote, arid, very, very hard, and quite perplexing. I would rather take the way out of myself.

So I regard my companion, the tree. And the solitude grows, warm and yet fearful, eternally quiet, only I am not a part of it.

The telephone rings.

2 *Sin and Licorice Candy Are Black,*

funeral shrouds and vanilla ice cream are white. May I have a little of both, please?

3 *Church and Race*

A white Christian, after visiting a Negro church, seemed generally pleased by the experience. Yet he expressed disappointment in the choir's performance. 'I don't understand it,' he said. 'The music was flat and very poor. With their natural sense of rhythm and good voices, I expected the music would be, well, you know, damned good. What happened?'

4

I find myself increasingly anti 'religion' and, at the same time, quite excited about the possibilities of a practised faith which can find expression in a life commitment. What solidifies my opposition to much of what passes as 'religion' is the idolatry surrounding it which seems actually to stand in the way of truly worshipping God. So seldom, within organized religion, does one encounter a non-watered-down, radical, offensive, joyful, maddeningly relevant presentation of the Christian gospel, coupled with an urgent resolve to translate the same gospel into personal and corporate life-style.

Instead, the gospel is apt to be presented at the most mundane, obscure and bland levels of academic dry rot. And, in the church life of organized religion, babies continue to be sprinkled with water in archaically irrelevant ceremonies in corners of churches at 4 P.M. on Sundays; society weddings go on their dreary way, aided and abetted by florists and photographers; the literally dead are given burial amid the stench of flowers, a treacly organ rendition of 'Abide with Me' and embarrassing public tears which have been emotionally induced by the very experience.

As a result of such things, many persons remain inside, as well as outside, the church *for the wrong reasons*. It is a wrong reason to remain outside because one has never faced the reality of the meaning of the church, as it is to remain inside a conveniently private club with economic, ethnic or racial qualifications for membership, along with a plaster Jesus.

Written by the author for 'Mademoiselle'

5

He is the only white in the room. About thirty black men and women are there too. He is now the focus of their attention. The atmosphere is poisoned by hate. He has felt this same hate among whites, only then he was not the lone black in their midst. Now he can't get his breath. Hate is reaching out to him, grabbing his hair and coat, stifling his mouth and nostrils, tugging to get him down on the floor. He sees hate in faces, hears it in words and silences, feels it looming up as a solid wall.

The demonic spirit takes on the form of white and black puppets killing each other in mock battle. Then it abruptly shifts to resemble sharp nails covering the floor. Humanness is still present but screams out for recognition. Blackness cries to whiteness: 'Unless you recognize my humanness, neither of us will be allowed to be human.'

Everyone in the room who is black has experienced, bitterly and precisely, what he is now facing as one mask confronted by a small army of reverse masks.

6 *P.R.*

Jeez, what a beautiful break! Page One! *And* a picture.

The controversy didn't get in. Isn't that great? Hey, Charlie, they left out the fight. Did you hear that? Isn't that great? Jeez, I was worried. I couldn't sleep all night. I thought, if they mention it – if they bring it into the story – then we've all got to live with it for a long, long time. But now it's over. This killed it.

That bastard, trying to argue at a public meeting. God, he'll be mad today. The story on the front page is just about the attainment awards and it uses four paragraphs from the official text of Joe's address.

So now everything's smooth. We can go on and build membership and expand our programme. It isn't the *time* for questioning goals. Why didn't the bastard know that? There's always some kook who's out to rock the boat, right, Charlie?

Jeez, we had a close shave. But Charlie – look! Isn't that story beautiful? Page One! *And* a picture!

7

A firecracker went off underneath my window. I jumped. It was a loud one. I was startled so that my heart pounded and I cried out. When I ran to the window, I saw two kids running as if the devil were after them.

Why *wouldn't* they shoot off a firecracker underneath an available window, I asked myself a moment later. They're normal kids. It's a holiday afternoon, hot, muggy, lazy. At least, this is what *we* used to do when I was their age.

Why should youngsters be grown-up before they grow up? Isn't there a place for a firecracker along with impersonal tall buildings, miles of city streets, and bumper-to-bumper traffic?

Yes. But still, I was startled, and *this* startles me.

8

I moved from one town to another and knew no one. I went out for football and wanted to make the team very much. This is the only time I have ever prayed. All I said was: God, help me get on that football team. It seemed to me that in that moment there was a greater strength in that bedroom of mine than me. I made the team. I do not believe in God.

Letter from a high-school student, after attending a church youth camp

9

The church has been killing prayer. Not only have they been cutting off communication with God, but they have been presenting a religious, set and conformed Christ, instead of the free Christ, full of life, who came to give us a joyous life, not one free of problems, but full of joy. This hurts me when I see the church trying to fit men into little moulds and say, 'Now you are acceptable. Now you are a Christian.'

Letter from a high-school student

Let's look, for a moment, at the reality of revolution, and fundamental structural changes within society. What this means for you today, in strategy and tactics, must be carefully thought out. If you should 'sell out', you would betray this revolution. You must continue to be abrasive, demanding, embarrassing, a veritable thorn in the society's flesh.

But you must accomplish this with a strategy in place of mere protest, infinite tact in place of mere (and easy) arrogance, substance in place of adventure.

Don't lead a slave revolt which doesn't work. Don't become a romantic, historical figure with a mystique. Make your revolution work. But you must understand the relationship between revolution *and* evolution. It is a luxury to become obsessed with self-righteousness. Remember that no institution, movement or person is without imperfections. Awareness of this reality permits dialogue between humans. When this is forgotten or deliberately (pridefully) overlooked, there can be no dialogue. There is no other kind of real communication. Then we have wars, higher walls of separation, more deeply engulfed ghettos, and the possibilities for holocaust.

Keep your revolution *human*. Will you try?

11

All my life I've been sick and tired. Now I'm sick and tired of being sick and tired.

Statement attributed to Mrs Fannie Lou Hamer, Congressional Challenger, Second District, Mississippi, 1964

12 *Alternatives Are Not 'Good' or 'Bad':*

They're 'Open' or 'Closed'.

13 *I Cannot Kiss Your Ring or Salute You*

You ask for my obedience. Earn it, then.

Who are you? Who am I? A lord and his servant, or men who are equally men? If you wish me to recognize your authority, show it to me in your*self*, your actions and style of being. Don't read any more words to me from statements you have composed in cool isolation and now seek to pronounce from a throne or platform.

Come down from your high place. Mingle with us, listen to us, speak to us without notes or a loudspeaker or a press agent as interpreter.

I will not honour your rank but only your person. I will not pay respect to your role, but only . . . *if* you earn it . . . to your*self*.

14 *The Telephone Is Absurdly Functional:*

It has only to ring.

15

I was now given up by the agent to the commanding officer at Fort Crawford, the White Beaver (General Atkinson) having gone down the river.

On our way down I surveyed the country that had cost us so much trouble, anxiety, and blood, and that now caused me to be a prisoner of war. I reflected upon the ingratitude of the whites when I saw their fine houses, rich harvests, and everything desirable around them; and recollected that all this land had been ours, for which I and my people had never received a dollar, and that the whites were not satisfied until they took our village and our graveyards from us and removed us across the Mississippi.

On our arrival at Jefferson Barracks we met the great war chief, White Beaver, who had commanded the American army against my little band. I felt the humiliation of my situation; a little while before I had been leader of my braves, now I was a prisoner of war. He received us kindly and treated us well.

We were now confined to the barracks and forced to wear the ball and chain. This was extremely mortifying and altogether useless. Was the White Beaver afraid I would break out of his barracks and run away? Or was he ordered to inflict this punishment upon me? If I had taken him prisoner on the field of battle I would not have wounded his feelings so much by such treatment, knowing that a brave war chief would prefer death to dishonour. But I do not blame the White Beaver for the course he pursued, as it is the custom among white soldiers and I suppose was a part of his duty.

From 'The Autobiography of Black Hawk'

16

A couple is seated at the next table in an expensive French restaurant.

The woman, who is talking in a deliberately high-pitched voice, has declined to order a drink. Her companion, with a note of desperation in his voice, has asked for a double martini on the rocks.

Could they be married? One thinks not. Could they be most unlikely lovers? Doubtful. Then who in heaven's name *can* they be? Delegates to a professional convention in the city, or faculty members at an urban university? (Yet what would they be doing *here*? Celebrating her tenure, or his dissertation? Both of them are at least forty.)

Now he has ordered another double martini on the rocks. She has asked for another glass of water.

She still speaks as if she were delivering a lecture or sermon.

Her voice is mannered and controlled. (Could anything throw her off guard?) He seems both embarrassed and matter-of-fact, as if this *has* happened before – the sortie into an expensive restaurant, her high-pitched observations, his outward compliance with an inner resistance (gin in the gut).

The couple at the next table: how strange they always seem!

17 *A Shiny, Sleek Black Limousine*

edges its way through throngs of people, in front of a luxury hotel. The driver asks the Great Lady if he may have the flower she is wearing on her suit to give to his wife. 'It would mean a lot to her,' he mutters, not quite lifting his eyes to look into her face. And she, the goddess, obliges by unfastening the flower and handing it to the driver.

'What a gracious thing to do,' someone says out loud. 'What a lovely thing for her to do.'

18 *Decision-Making Is the Great Issue*

Deal me in, man. Damn it, deal me in.

19 *Conversation With a Little Girl*

Interviewer: Tell me something about you – where you were born, you know, where you grew up, how everything went for you?

Gwen D: When I was born I lived on 118th Street. There was a man killed in the hallway, and a man died right in front of the door where I lived at. My mother after that man got killed. I liked it in 97th Street because it was integration in that block. All kinds of people lived there.

Interviewer: Spanish people? White people?

Gwen D: Spanish people, Italian people, all kinds of people. I liked it because it wasn't one group of whites and one group of Negroes or Spanish or something like that; everybody who lived in that block were friends.

Interviewer: How come you moved?

Gwen D: Well, my mother she didn't like the building too well.

Interviewer: What didn't she like about it?

Gwen D: Well, it was falling down!

Interviewer: In your whole life, has anything happened to you that you really got excited about?

Gwen D: I can't remember.

Interviewer: Tell me about some real good times you've had in your life.

Gwen D: In Harlem?

Interviewer: In your life, that you've really enjoyed.

Gwen D: One year we was in summer school, and we went to this other school way downtown, out of Harlem, to give a show, and everybody was so happy. And we were on television, and I saw myself, and I was the only one there with a clean skirt and blouse.

Interviewer: And you really got excited about that. Anything else ever happen to you that you had a really good time?

Gwen D: No.

Interviewer: What kind of changes would you want to make? Changes so that you can have a better chance, your sisters can have a better chance and your brother?

Gwen D: Well, I just want a chance to do what I can.

From 'Dark Ghetto' by Kenneth B. Clark

20

I am a thirty eight-year-old, protestant, southern, housewife and mother of three children. I have gone to church all my life, until recently, but somehow, they keep pushing Jesus away.

So I took my kids out of the church and I left too. We have to find out about Jesus some other way.

I've learned something. Jesus is white, Negro, yellow, red, Jew. I wish I didn't know that. I live in the wrong place, at the wrong time, to know it. Pray for me. It's too big, I'm scared and lonely. I can't do anything but teach this to the kids and try to have the guts to say and live it as opportunity comes. All of the children can help. It just has to be better in the next generation. Can we learn to see persons, and can our hearts be taught to love?

Letter from a housewife

21 A Prayer

I tried hard to practise nonviolence, Jesus.

I really tried, but it's not easy at all. Those of us who marched in the picket line gathered at around noon. The policeman assigned to keep order told us how far we could march in each direction, and asked us to keep the centre of the sidewalk open so other people could get through easily.

One guy tried to start an argument by shouting at us and calling us names. Most people going by, walking or in cars, were indifferent. A few looked angrily at us and some others smiled or waved. One woman shouted an encouraging greeting from her car.

It's hard getting out on a picket line and demonstrating in front of everybody, Lord. There's such an empty, awful feeling of being isolated from the rest of the world when you're out there on a picket line.

I felt I had to do this today, Jesus. I can't stand back and avoid getting involved. Please get inside all our hearts, those of us out on the picket line and the people on the other side of it. Please bring us together. And, Jesus, please let us have peace.

Students stood around holding beer cans and smoking cigarettes. The blazing sun was beating down on the boardwalk overlooking the ocean at Daytona Beach, Florida. It was Good Friday afternoon and I was conducting a service for several hundred of the 50,000 students who had come to the Florida city for the annual spring vacation trek.

I read a poem about the crucifixion by Ferlinghetti; told the princess's story from Tennessee Williams' *Sweet Bird of Youth*; read the experience of a Jewish psychiatrist, Viktor E. Frankl, in a Nazi concentration camp, and the letter written by a Scandinavian cabin boy following his torture by the Nazis (Kim's letter in *Dying We Live*); and related the feeling of pain and despair felt by a couple in Kenya that their intimacy might result in the birth of yet another black baby who would suffer in white society (recounted by Louis Lomax in *The Reluctant African*).

The students knew about the world's sufferings. Underneath their deadpan expressions and hippy jargon, there was a terrible search for meaning. They have inherited the legacy of double-standard morality, anti-Semitism, racial prejudice, war-as-usual, ethical hypocrisies and the separation of religion from life. (Ironically – because I was accompanied to Daytona Beach in 1963 by a racially integrated group of four – only one hotel or motel accommodation, seven miles from the centre of the city, was available to us. It was necessary for us to rent a car for transportation. We could dine only at our motel, a local lunch counter, or another restaurant belonging to a national chain. The legacy which society had given the students was quite obviously all around us!)

Students will not, under any circumstances, accept packaged answers from anybody to questions they have not asked. They demand the right to ask whatever questions they wish. Only when they have done this, is it possible for them to engage with their 'teachers' in an honest dialogue about life. And dialogue it must be.

23

We dined with her on Thanksgiving Day. She was a very greedy old lady, and had supplied a feast which required a gargantuan stomach. Just as we were about to eat the first mouthful, she said: 'Let us pause and think of the poor.' Apparently she found this thought an appetizer.

From 'The Autobiography of Bertrand Russell'

24 Jesus Had a Penis

In his thirty-three years, as God and man, Jesus had a head, shoulders, stomach, penis, legs and feet.

What's so shocking about this? Nothing, really. The only shocking thing is the reaction of certain people to it.

First, some people consider 'penis' a dirty word; the body is evil; in polite 'Christian' society one is not supposed to acknowledge physical realities, only spiritual ones. 'Christianity', some people say, does not consider the body or mind of man. but only his soul. In fact, taking this point of view, 'Christianity' is not concerned with society, politics, economics, the arts or sociology; it is about 'religion'.

Secondly, some people consider Jesus to be God but not man. Well, yes, maybe Man, but not man. He could never have had a penis (though the Latin American church observes a day of the holy foreskin). Okay, maybe he did have a penis, but don't *talk* about it.

Don't talk about Jesus as real. Keep him up there in the sky where he's uninvolved in real, raw life. The 'Christians' who don't want to talk about Jesus's penis, strangely, seem to live in restricted neighbourhoods where Jews and Negroes can't rent or buy homes. My God, what *is* profane?

25 "Hippie"

He said it, and a change came over his face. He was no longer a genial, civic-minded, churchgoing, small-town bank president. He actually seemed to be hating something or someone.

'Hippie,' he expostulated. 'Communists with smelly bodies and matted hair. I'd have the police round them up and beat hell out of them.'

He was speaking quietly but with a scratchy intensity. The room was very silent – silence accentuated by a clock ticking in the hall and a fire crackling in the grate. Outside snow was gently falling.

26 Street Scene

Three women appear to be figures by Giacometti.

One woman speaks to the others as they begin to move apart: 'Where we gonna meet?'

There is no response, not even indifference. The woman asks again: 'Where we gonna meet?'

Now they are frozen. A decision will have to be made. Yet the three figures do not move. The woman asks again: 'Where we gonna meet?'

The sun is shining on the street. A breeze is blowing. Other figures move. There is the sound of automobiles and other voices.

'Where we gonna meet?'

27 Where God Is

Some people have very definite ideas about where God is. I recall speaking about evangelism, of all things, to a group of suburbanites in an inner-city church building where they meet once a week. Otherwise they never go near the place and want nothing at all to do with anybody who lives in the neighbourhood, which is a poor one. Evangelism (for them) concerns India, Brazil and Ghana. I happened to ask these evangelistic people if they had ever been inside the tavern across the street from the church. They reacted in shock and not a little anger. 'You're here to talk about *evangelism*,' someone reproved me. So God couldn't be in the tavern. Then, precisely, where would He be?

From 'Our Prayers are meaningless,' written by the author for 'The Saturday Evening Post'

28 *At the Flicks:* Georgy Girl

She resides in a world where the Beatles are surely more popular than Jesus. Yes, Jesus loves Georgy Girl.

29

An age which is essentially restless and at odds with itself finds that in the work of Picasso that same restlessness is consecrated and turned to great account and those inner divisions externalized and exploited, one by one, as sources of energy and power. People who would in themselves fear to remark even that tiny part of the world which concerns them directly find in Picasso the example of a man who has been re-making his world, and our world, for the past sixty years; and, mysteriously, some part of his downrightness and insensitivity to fear is communicated to ourselves. That is the point of Picasso; and that is why, in honouring him, we do honour to ourselves.

From 'The Importance of Picasso' by John Russell

30 *A Young Black Nationalist Said:*

'I don't know what to say about the future. I don't know what to tell whites they should do. I'm not sure it can make any difference any more.'

But he concluded: 'I wish whites would listen. I wish whites could hear.'

31

My deepest experience I had in Tennessee, where I got immediately mixed up in a racial controversy. I took the part of a Negro who was refused a cup of coffee at the buffet of the bus depot. I spent three hours with him. The whites looked furious, the black people more curiously upon us. And afterwards, again and again, I got just sick by seeing what is involved in being either white or black. Sometimes I might paint myself black for being able to share. However, it might be my suffering in not being allowed to share in that way, which might be too easy; it may be I will just have to experience what it means to find no place at all, neither in the front nor at the bottom of the scene which is called life, and to walk as a stranger between black and white. I will have to accept this suffering as a white man who receives what his race almost carefully prepared, and as a Christian who knows what place his Lord found when He came to visit His people in humility. . . .

Letter from a European monk who, during a visit to the United States in 1957, took a bus trip through some Southern States. From 'The Hunger, the Thirst' by the author

JUNE

1 The Question of Communication

once drove me nearly to distraction. Words were obviously mere subterfuges, being outshouted by actions; anyway, people seemed to use words as sophisticated means of keeping each other at arm's length and thereby avoiding any real, painful, honest communication. Deeds may seem to replace words when occasionally some people are fools enough to believe in deeds as if they could be pure and holy.

They can't. Deeds are laced through with moral ambiguities, mixed motives, historical sins, social outrages and personal egotisms. But an awareness of the limitation of deeds, along with a sense of the futility of words, does not mean an end of communication. It seems, on the other hand, to signal a beginning – a beginning of a real hope of communication. For it is the *being there*, the being with another person or persons in a situation when one is involved, that opens up a possibility of communication which could not have existed when one was relying on gimmicks and good faith. Now it is publicly confessed that one stands in guilt and fear, without resources or a panacea; one can bring nothing to another but himself, and be willing and in need to receive the other; so, in the silence of this awareness, there may be a beginning of communication.

2 You See This Watch

A Negro, around fifty, was talking to a group of White Establishment leaders in the Mississippi town in which he had lived his entire life. 'You can destroy it and the watch factory, too, but you can't destroy time.' A few nights earlier, some angry whites had fired gunshots into his home; bullet holes riddled the front screen door and the wallpaper on the bedroom wall. He continued telling the white leaders: 'And you can kill me and wipe out my family, but you can't stop the freedom movement.'

3

Can we Christians stay where we are and work for good, or should we go out and look in the 'gutters'?

Letter from a woman

4

In meeting with church officials, you find a profound suspicion of the fact that God is not only in the church but is present everywhere in the world as the Lord of history. These officials think and live on the basis that God is present only in the church, with perhaps some dim idea that he is somehow remotely involved in the world.

Comments made by a prominent European theologian

5

Next major institution headed for massive demythologizing: Marriage.

6

Ashes to dust,
        dust to ashes,
        but let the spirit burn.

7 *You Can't Stand Up and Thunder Negatives*

but you can try the give-and-take of an open, honest dialogue. Sure, you may end up being called a kook. That's fine.

There's a terrible need for a great many more liberals to *rock* the boat instead of talking about it.

8

Of late, I find myself increasingly dissatisfied with traditional answers to moral questions. I have recently realized that I don't know what can be said to the homosexual by the Christian without sounding hard and cruel.

The traditional answer of the church seems so useless and seems to place Jesus Christ so far from these people. What is it that Jesus Christ can bring to the homosexual?

I hope you do not think it an intrusion for me to ask you these things. I know no ministers or priests with whom these questions can be discussed. For me, if I come to feel my faith is meaningless in any one area of life, it is in great danger of becoming completely meaningless.

Letter from a university professor

9 *Letter to the Author Postmarked San Diego, California*

boyd:
You filthy scum – your attempt to shame the 'cloth' by turning your collar will gain you little but contempt from the white race and the blacks are only using you for their catspaw and will spit on you after your usefulness is over, under the blanket they KNOW you are a traitor and trust you even less than they do the white man who openly shows his true feelings, at least HE is honest.

Verman as yourself will be delt with by our Lord when HE sickens with your scorn of HIM, nothing but HIS great compassion and pity permits your survival, I wonder just how you feel when ALONE and look in the mirror at your self, another Judas.

You make me want to throw-up, on you.

A white Christian

10 *Pike County*

On July 8, 1964, at about 3.40 A.M., I was asleep in a bed which was about 2½ feet away from the window. A bomb was placed about 1½ feet from the outside of the window.

I don't recall hearing any noise. I only remember lying on the floor beside my bed under glass from the window and the lumber from the window frame.

I assume that I had been unconscious for some time, for everyone had already made it to safety by the time I realized what had happened.

When I finally made it to safety (the kitchen) I was still dazed and noticed that I was bleeding profusely. I later learned that my body was covered with small cuts, and some thirty of them were deep cuts.

I believe the house . . . was bombed because it was occupied by myself and other COFO workers and was being used as a Freedom House. My home is in Summit, Mississippi. I am a citizen of the United States of America.

Signed: Curtis Hayes
From 'Mississippi Black Paper'

11 *The Typewriter*

Type fast, type so fast that you must think fast, type faster, think faster. The important letters written on the typewriter and the unimportant letters. 'Please turn off the utilities for two months.' 'I guess this is the last letter I will write. Good-bye.' 'I am applying for a new job.' 'I hope that you will consider me seriously for this job.' 'I am lonely and I miss you.'

12

Communication is by telephone calls, improvised luncheon meetings attended by people who have cut an important conference session, and letter-writing (my guess would be that the key to America's future lies somewhere in private letters).

From 'American Theology, Radicalism and the Death of God' by William Hamilton

13

A mother walks into a bedroom to find her baby being bitten by a rat; when the mother approaches, the rat attacks her ... a housewife looks up to find a rat wedged in a hole in the kitchen ceiling; she calls in a cop; he refuses to touch it ... a grandmother's orphaned grand-daughter is confined in a state institution because in the atmosphere of her rat-plagued apartment, the child's attacks of asthma quickly return ... during a TV newscast on slum conditions, a daughter turns to her mother and asks, 'Mama, we don't live in a house like that, do we?'; at precisely that moment, there is a crash from behind a door; the bathroom ceiling has just fallen in ... a family is driven out of its apartment in the middle of the winter when water from a broken upstairs pipe floods the kitchen ... a woman's leg is scarred by bites from 'them big black water bugs'. ...

In dead of winter, with no heat in the house, dangerous electric heaters share the children's sleeping rooms ... trash and garbage lie uncollected in the halls ... and there is the omnipresent, penetrating stench of urine.

These are some of the manifold horrors of slum living. They

were all actually observed during no more than half-a-dozen excursions into the blight of just two cities (New York and Washington).

From 'The Shame of a Nation' by Philip M. Stern and George de Vincent

14 *A Paradox*

Power must be defined in terms of weakness, and weakness in terms of power.

(What is each?)

15 *Why Am I Afraid?*

There is a small grain of terror somewhere inside me. I'm frightened that it might grow, absorb other particles of myself, and overcome me. Some day I may find no solid ground on which to move, or feel, or relate. I may just sink down.

I seem to be afraid of people, especially people I love and am quite close to. Why? It seems this terror in me reaches out to them. I am afraid I will find no solid ground in them when I need it most. I fear that a shadow will be where a person should, and, reaching out for a hand or arm or shoulder, I will grasp a shadow's ghostly form.

I don't want to be afraid.

16 *Free Press*

The student newspaper editor has been fired. He insisted on ferreting out the truth about a controversial issue that reached all the way up to the president's office. He found what he was looking for, made a decision to print it, and now he's out.

The campus is caught up in one of those brief tornadoes which will make a storm today and become folklore tomorrow. Yes, there are 'results', but they are hidden now. A dean of students will quietly resign next spring after a long winter of not quite managing will add this incident to that mosaic which will, four years hence, loom up and tell him to become an ex-professor. The college president's wife won't have sex with her husband for five months, three weeks and four days. The student editor will, within five years, base his dissertation on the incident.

But today there is only sadness, discussion and brief fury. Students are holding a rally to demand a free press on campus (the rally is, however, much smaller than the crowd drawn by a folk-song group), the hard-core younger faculty dissident group is drinking beer at the home of an assistant professor of English and planning new strategy, and a tame issue of the student newspaper, under the watchful eye of the head of the journalism department, is going to press.

17

Why does the top of the Washington monument
resemble a Ku Klux Klan symbol, with two eyes seeming
to peer out of a white Kleagle's hood?
(Research! Research!)

18 *He's a Communist!*

Sir, why do you say that?

Because he's a nigger-lover, kike-lover-son-of-a-bitch, and he's making trouble. He's stirring up the niggers and the kikes and the YOUTH. He's a Communist.

Sir, do you mean he's a follower of Marx?

Who's Marx? What are you talking about? Are *you* a Commie too? I mean, goddamnit, he's an atheist son-of-a-bitch who's attacking the power structure and stirring up the YOUTH and upsetting things the way they always have been.

But, sir . . .

You're asking too damn many questions. I think you're a Jew-Commie and an anti-Christian, anti-American bastard yourself. Don't ask *questions*, goddamnit. It's *answers* we've got to give the people if we're going to get back to the old way of life.

19

Tired
And lonely,
So tired
The heart aches.
Meltwater trickles
Down the rocks,
The fingers are numb,
The knees tremble.
It is now,
Now that you must not give in.

On the path of the others
Are resting places,
Places in the sun
Where they can meet.
But this
Is your path,
And it is now,
Now, that you must not fail.

Weep
If you can,
Weep,
But do not complain.
The way chose you –
And you must be thankful.

From 'Markings' by Dag Hammarskjold

83

20 *At the Flicks:* 8½

What does it mean to start over again in one's life? It is a possibility that some of us have to consider.

21

Why is the sun so red as it sets tonight?
Is it gorged with the blood of men who died today in war?

22

This is *serious* drinking.

Drown out the seashell music, blot out all the pain, make a new pain which can be *felt* to take the place of the other.

Death, are you quiet or loud?

You frighten me, yet I feel I could embrace you in this moment of pain and fury. You couldn't hurt me more than I am hurt. You couldn't depress me more than I am depressed.

But don't come. Stay wherever you are.

I know you're close. I feel your not breathing. I hear your heart not beating. In pain, I still want the aching restlessness of a heartbeat. In fury, the unbridled movement of breath. Don't come.

23

'I'm worried that he may commit suicide,' she said.

I knew about his insecurity, personal problems and very real feeling of hopelessness. For him, there seemed to be little ahead but the same straight, unrelenting hard road: no turns, travel day and night, no destination.

Precisely what was he feeling? Obliteration seemed to crowd out all the people and events in his life. How had he got jammed into himself to the point of this malaise? Without silly pep talks, how could we get him to see out of his two eyes?

He was deeply religious, active in church and an avid reader of theology. Evidently, the link between these things and his life had been shattered. Perhaps it had never been there at all. For what he lacked, it seemed, was plain and simple meaning.

24

They hate people. They are fed up working with people they think of as pigs, always caught in the same dirty problems and dilemmas. Can you tell them any reason why they should love people? Can you give them any basis for feeling there is dignity in man?

Invitation to address a group of volunteer workers in a poverty programme

25 Salvation

She's a housewife. Marijuana, LSD and such (to her) glamorous commodities will not help at all. But she feels that a cigarette will, along with her cup of coffee. 'I need a drag. I'm kind of insecure and nervous,' she says. 'I need to hold something in my hand.'

Downtown, her husband can't have a Gibson until lunch. But he needs some kind of lift. 'This is a crowded room and there are a lot of people I don't know. I feel self-conscious. I just need to relax. I'm so damned tense and that last hour was real hell. I have to let go somehow. Maybe a cigarette will help.

26

Through the slits in an old wooden fence.

I suddenly realize I am looking at a tree, which appears to be cut into neat green slices.

27 A Sophisticated, Liberal White Woman

is chatting with me over a drink after I have given an address at an annual Urban League dinner. She is speaking of the executive secretary of the Urban League, who is a Negro. 'If only all Negroes were like Bill,' she whispers to me, smiling in his direction across the room, 'there'd be no *problem.*'

28 A Prayer

I'm down and out, Jesus. I've tried and tried and tried and I just come up with the same no go.

Everything I've looked at today, everything I've thought about, I've just related the whole bit to *me*. Me. I want to get out of my damned shell, Lord. I want to get out with the people, out there, Jesus, outside myself.

But I come back and sit in my shell and vomit and, frankly, Jesus, I'm disgusted with myself. Take me out of myself, Lord.

I know you're merciful. So have mercy on me today, okay? Give me some of your mercy right now, okay?

29

His own father was beaten to death with a hammer by a railroad guard. And they brought his father home like that. My mother got frightened, she wanted my father to pray. And he said, he shouted it at the top of his lungs, Pray? *Who*, pray? I bet you, if I ever get anywhere near that white devil you call God, I'll tear my son and my father out of his white hide. Don't you never say that word Pray to me again, woman, not if you want to *live*. Then he started to cry. I'll never forget it. Maybe I hadn't loved him before, but I loved him then. That was the last time he ever shouted, he hasn't raised his voice since.

From 'Another Country' by James Baldwin

30 When I Played "the hungry i":

Nothing in recent years intrigued me more than the uproar which greeted me when I read my prayers and meditations, and replied informally and openly to people's questions, as a paid performer in a San Francisco nightclub.

Man had indeed bitten dog. Certain critics were furious. 'Get back inside your damned cathedrals and lousy churches,' they demanded. 'Don't mix things up. You're a priest; quit crawling around outside your ghetto. You've got your role, priest; stick to it. Don't get involved in *life*. *Your* field is religion, Father. Stay with your Jesus inside a cathedral. We don't want any Jesus stuff out here where the air is blowing and issues are real.'

A newspaper cartoon showing a father getting ready for church on a Sunday morning. His small son was asking him: 'Where are we going, Dad? St Paul's or the hungry i?' One lady asked me: 'Do you really feel you bring Jesus with you into the hungry i?' I could only reply: 'I don't *bring* Jesus anywhere. I just join him where he is.'

One night, during my appearance at the hungry i, two people got up and walked out. Shortly afterwards, in the course of the question-and-answer period, a man asked me: 'Why do you think those people walked out on you? Did they disapprove of what you are doing?' Frankly, I didn't know. But a note handed to me cleared up the matter. It had been left with a waiter, and read: 'My apologies for leaving, but we are students and my date must return to the dorm before midnight. Many thanks.'

I suppose the most poignant memento of the hungry i is some words, scrawled in pencil on a paper napkin, which were handed to me after I had read a meditation from my book *Free to Live, Free to Die*, beginning with the words: 'A smokestack means burned bodies.' The meditation concerns violence in modern society, with particular reference to Nazi concentration camps, torture in Algeria and lynchings in America. On the paper napkin, I saw: 'Chimney – that's what it meant once, Jesus – don't let it have any other meaning again.'

JULY

1 *The Beginning of Charity:*

There's no 'them'.

2 *To My Dog and My Cat*

If the truth were known, I like you equally well.

This is not to say you are in the least the same.

One of you is quite patient with me, hardly ever selfish (except at mealtimes), very easy to live with (although surprisingly easily hurt), and always around to meet my every need.

The other is easily put-out and impatient with me, extremely self-centred and selfish (therefore, mysterious and puzzling), awfully complicated to live with . . . but never boring, absent on a whim, secretive, and making me aware of meeting *your* every need.

One of you invariably makes a good, firm, steady impression on guests, obeys orders, retreats when commanded, and sleeps as late as I do in the morning.

The other can, with malice aforethought, make a most sinister impression on guests, even frighten them. You can callously disobey orders, cling on to guests who find in you the very incarnation of a medieval devil, and wake me up at dawn by getting up on my pillow and purring.

One of you wags a tail in devotion, the other rotates a tail in anger. One of you licks my hand as a sign of affection, the other sits on my lap and scratches my knee, even to the point of drawing my blood, equally affectionate.

Both of you have four legs, are the same colour, take an afternoon nap and possess healthy appetites. I must bathe one of you, whereas the other attends personally to such an intimate matter.

Each of you is something of an intellectual, I think, and also has a hard core of integrity. You know very well when you have done the right or the wrong thing. You are both capable of the worst mischief and the greatest kindness.

I like you equally well . . . one at a time. One of you is like salt, the other pepper. There is a moment and a place for you both. I'd rather not mix my moments and places, and, for once, you *both* agree with me.

3

'My boss is white,' said Simple.

'Most bosses are,' I said.

'And being white and curious, my boss keeps asking me just what does THE Negro want. Yesterday he tackled me during the coffee break, talking about THE Negro. He always says "THE Negro", as if there was not 50-11 different kinds of Negroes in the U.S.A.,' complained Simple. 'My boss says, "Now that you-all have got the Civil Rights Bill and the Supreme Court, Adam Powell in Congress, Ralph Bunche in the United Nations, and Leontyne Price singing in the Metropolitan Opera, plus Dr Martin Luther King getting the Nobel Prize, what more do you want? I am asking you, just what does THE Negro want?"

'"I am not THE Negro," I says. "I am *me*."'

From 'Simple's Uncle Sam' by Langston Hughes

4

I did not have to read books to know that the theme of life is conflict and pain. Instinctively, all my clowning was based on this.

From 'My Autobiography' by Charles Chaplin

5

'I'm so tired today. I've been pushing much too hard and need to rest.'

'Good Lord, you'd *better*. What did you do yesterday?'

'I flew from California.'

6

I'm finding myself becoming progressively more radical. It scares me mainly because the more I see how drastic change must be in this country, the more convinced I am that it will only be accompanied by great suffering. Also I am coming to see how easy it is to hate, especially when one feels frustrated and powerless. How do you live with the knowledge of the hypocrisy and evil our government and the American people are doing and are capable of doing?

I keep coming to the same old question, asked in many different ways – how do we stay human, become human and work for a world in which people can be human?

Letter from a college student

7

Second Negro: Damn whites. Dirty whiggers. Dirty whiggers.
First Negro: I've asked you not to use that term in speaking about whites, Art. I find it offensive.

From 'They aren't Real to Me', an unpublished play by the author

8 *Turning on to the Flicks:*

The old Bette Davis, Olivia de Havilland, Humphrey Bogart, Ginger Rogers, Ida Lupino, Ingrid Bergman films – in thousands of homes and apartments across the land, late at night; while these flicker across TV tubes in darkened rooms, it's time to turn on, baby.

9 A Bishop Commented

that he has two kinds of clergy serving under him: the dead and the deeply disturbed. He hopes he may always belong to the latter group.

10 Party

Joe took another drink and listened to Jimmy Dixon. Dixon was burlesquing an old ballad by making it dirty and the crowd seemed to love it, although it was smart to smile at the person on your right as if to say, 'Poor Jimmy! Christ, he's drunk, isn't he? A character . . . but he belongs.'

Then Joe saw Doris Dixon. She was sitting a few feet away, her legs crossed and her skirt up too high. But otherwise she was quite proper, wearing black with not too much, not too little, jewellery. Joe walked over and sat down by her. Jimmy was singing loudly and the piano was loud, but they could hear each other very well.

Doris had married Jimmy in New York when he was just starting up the ladder. He was corny but likeable, ambitious and very sober, to boot. They fell in love. Joe thought, sitting by her, that Doris was still very much in love with Jimmy, although he was usually too far gone to care or else was latched down with the TV singer he liked. Jimmy was still corny and still likeable, in a caricatured sort of way, but he was no longer ambitious – why should he be? – and definitely no longer sober.

'Hello, Joe. Good to see you,' she said in her very sincere way, looking at him with her big black eyes and smiling as much as she was able. She was half-crocked. Joe was too by that time. But he knew she was.

'Hi, Doris. Having a good time, honey?' he asked her.
'Good time?'

11 *Tradition*

Once I served in a beautiful church. Many people would not have thought it beautiful because it was very old, and located in a slum, and simple to a fault. It had white brick walls, black wooden pews, old windows and an altar.

But over the altar hung an immense wooden figure of Jesus, suffering on the cross. I felt that it belonged there in the penitential church seasons of Advent and Lent, but not the rest of the year. A triumphant Christ on the cross, or an empty cross, would have been closer to the meaning of the gospel. However, I was told that my removing the nailed-up Christ would result in a mass defection of people from the parish. *Tradition*. I well remember the Easter when I preached about why I wanted to move the tortured Jesus from over the altar, but couldn't. The reaction to the sermon was no reaction.

And there was the week when someone had some extra red paint. It was suggested that we paint the door of the church red to spruce it up and give us all a new sense of the colour and vigour of God's kingdom. We painted it. Suddenly we were plunged into sharp and bitter controversy – *not* about the virgin birth or the Trinity, *not* about poverty, race or peace, but about *the red door*.

12 *The Newspaper*

answers the questions we so insistently ask, 'what's new?' or 'what's happening?'

'I want to know all about it. The reason I like a newspaper is that I don't like just surface news, I don't want to know just superficial facts about people and things, I want to know *all* about them; and the newspaper does provide depth coverage, doesn't it? Here I am reading this morning about Grace Kelly and Prince Rainier, and it's nice to know all about them, they're so interesting, and to have real depth in my understanding of them. Married all those years. Imagine, being the princess. And it's all here, here in the newspaper.'

13 The Fantasy Nigger World

where lightness was darkness, men were things, hope was wretched, and love was some ashes beneath a charred piece of rope on a tree. Where black men were despised by white men, a black woman felt anguish stir inside her in the form of another black baby who must be maimed and tortured by a white Christian world, a black child learned the hate stare as he first felt the sharp stones of the ghetto wall, a white god blessed the status quo, a white Christ came to men only in the form of a white host in the sacrament, white angels sang with joy over the manger scene, and blackness was sin, death, a night without stars, a tenement, a segregated school, a job for whites only, and degradation, degradation, degradation.

14

For a voyage to a destination, wherever it may be, is also a voyage inside oneself; even as a cyclone carries along with it the centre in which it must ultimately come to rest. At these moments I think not only of the places I have been to but also of the distances I have travelled within myself without friend or ship; and of the long way yet to go before I come home within myself and within the journey.

From 'Venture to the Interior' by Laurens van der Post

15

HOW IS IT POSSIBLE
to pray for victory in war?
DOES THIS MEAN
there is a tribal god who loves one side while hating the other?
AND DOES THIS MEAN
the tribal god is a dispenser of quick, ugly magic that can kill?
(*And* what *does* victory *mean?*)

16 *At the Flicks:* Morgan!

Could 1984 be *your* year?

17 *'A White Cop*

stopped my car to give me a ticket the other day,' a Negro
woman relates. 'He just stood there and told me: "Get out,
nigger bitch." I'm not going to take that any more from the
blue-eyed devil.'

18

What shall we tell the American poor, once we have seen
them? Shall we say to them that they are better off than the
Indian poor, the Italian poor, the Russian? That is one answer,
but it is heartless. I should put it another way. I want to tell
every optimistic and well-fed American that it is intolerable
that so many millions should be maimed in body and spirit when
it is not necessary that they should be. My standard of comparison is not how much worse things used to be. It is how
much better they could be if only we were stirred.

From 'The Other America' by Michael Harrington

95

19

I have the feeling of living in a machine which produces effectively, but it is dangerous to slow down at all, and fatal to stop, because one will be crushed by other little, whirling wheels like oneself.

Letter from a middle-aged man

20

Once my minister said grace over a milkshake. Don't you think this is carrying it too far? I know I should follow the minister's example, but how can I go to a party and say grace over the punch.

Query from a teen-age girl

21 *It's a Double-Feature in the Drive-in Movie*

It's late, so a lot of couples aren't seeing what's up on the screen anyway.

But it's one of those dumpy SEX (say it again) SEX movies which come out of Hollywood in unmarked tin cans and aren't sexy. I mean, they've got dames and crooners and some corn-ball double-edged jokes and even a few SEX (say it again) SEX scenes which fade out before they actually get sexy.

Yet nothing up there on the screen is sexy. It's just supposed to be because that's the way it's advertised. Actually, it's kind of small-town smutty and behind-the-barn four-letter-word dirty, you know? It never grew up. There's no real sex up there on the screen. It's down here in the cars.

22

'The black bourgeoisie has sold out the whole freedom movement,' a black Chicago militant said. 'Don't mention bourgeois to me. And we don't need any white man to help us or tell us what to do, or how to do it. All a white man can say now is, "Let me listen, let me hear, tell the facts, let me experience it as it is." I don't want to be a part of any white world. It's rotten and it stinks. Why should *I* be corrupted by *it*? I want a new and decent world. I don't trust whites. I think the motives of all whites in the movement are sick, man. I'm tired of paternalism, especially when it acts humble and Christian. But guns won't win the war. Only education will, and that means dollars.'

23

What is a typical teen-ager these days? You have a lot of problems so you tell somebody about them and they call you a typical teen-ager. I don't believe there is such a thing.

Letter from a teen-age student

24 *Notes of a College Chaplain*

The college chaplain scene was pretty bad. Dollhouse denominational centres (mine being one of these) were scattered about the fringes of the campus, resembling cute ecclesiastical additions to a monopoly set. Inside each segregated ghetto, one could miraculously find 'a home away from home', complete with cheap spaghetti suppers and bathroom facilities away from the Student Union. Accompanying this was withdrawal into a self-centred web of personal piety, with emphasis on sin and salvation as personal (*me – me – me – my* God *my – sin – my* salvation).

Somewhat logically, this led the church to the burgeoning, healthy coffeehouse movement. Church coffeehouses often became simply the church playing church by candlelight over red-checked tablecloths, with the same people talking to the same people. In this spirit came jazz masses (often with in-excusably poor jazz), which, as bread and circuses, provided some kicks but took people's minds off of fundamental problems which remained unmet. An avant-garde 'image'! A great problem of the jazz and folk masses is that they set old words to new music, whereas the deeper need was for *new words* to new music.

25

The deep questions which torment and plague us are almost laughably simple ones. They concern only living and dying. All of us do both of these things.

1-2-3-4-5-6: simple, we say.

4-1-6-3-5-2: complex, paradoxical, irrational, jagged, the jungle, 'the abyss'!

From a foreword by the author in 'The People on Second Street' by Jenny Moore

26 A Prayer

It's a night spot, Jesus.

Yet it seems more like a church than many churches. I mean, there's a real sense of community. People are humanly relating to each other, Lord. Nothing here seems rigid or pre-arranged. The action is spontaneous.

I think the music is holier than the music in many churches. It's not a hymn out of another century, Jesus. This music isn't built on old images. It doesn't suggest an ancient view of life that is remote from what people are feeling. Instead it frees people and causes them to relate. It's *now*.

Thanks, Jesus, for the possibility of free action which I find here. Thanks for being here with us.

27 *The Party Last Night Was a Success*

It was also a rather good party. But it seems almost to have been scripted and directed. Is that why it was a Success? The drinks were fine, the buffet irreproachable, the guest list a fascinating combination of very important names. But, damn it, the whole thing was a production. Why couldn't the hosts have risked a happening?

28 *Film*

the hidden world.

I'm going to sit down in the darkened theatre. Then I'm going right up there to the big screen and walk through it. I'm going to meet Audrey Hepburn when I walk into that other life. I'm going to talk with Audrey Hepburn. I like Miss Hepburn and think I know her quite well.

I certainly don't want her to die, but if she has to, I'll bet it will be beautiful and I want to be right there. It will be so cool and real, you know?

29

We've talked a great deal about jail. Although it frightens me to think of Claude in jail for a few years, I know that it would be better than the Army. Claude is not a pacifist but he knows that once in the Armed Services he will have no civil rights and that his right to protest and refuse to cooperate with what he considers evil actions by our government will be denied him and that, therefore, refusal once in will carry a heavier penalty. And because he already opposes the war completely, he knows that he might as well make his stand now.

Letter from a young wife

30 *Baroque*

is now the studied appearance of simplicity.

31 *We were Driving in a Car in the South in 1962*

We had been involved all day in a sit-in at a restaurant. We had not been served ... there were five of us, three whites and two Negroes. We passed a hot-dog stand: yes, we could get hot dogs there and eat them in the car. 'Why not drive to the airport restaurant? It's integrated. It will make us feel human. We can be served there.' We sat in the car, driving fast on the highway; it was night and we were very hungry, too hungry even to try to keep a conversation going. We just drove, and it was very dark and we were out in the country. Then suddenly the airport, bright lights flashing out over the night. The restaurant had closed five minutes before we arrived.

AUGUST

1 *She's One of the World's Richest Women*

The morning newspaper said so.

How rich, I wonder. (How rich was Kublai Khan, Louis XIV, Catherine the Great, Lorenzo the Magnificent, John D. Rockefeller, Henry Ford?) Her name isn't nearly so interesting as Gulbenkian, but much more so than J. Paul Getty. (Does Getty stem from 'get' or 'getting?' What is the significance of the mysterious J.?) Gulbenkian is almost as fascinating as the Begum Aga Khan (*she's* terribly rich, according to the Sunday supplements and news magazines).

All those General Motors executives are richer than Croesus but uninterestingly anonymous. (Ralph Nader is better known; one can have celebrity without riches).

However, celebrity *with* riches is considered preferable. Aristotle Onassis. (I think the name, under the circumstances, cannot be topped.) He is a Mont Blanc among the world's richest. The Texas rich (whom, they say, are *very* rich) are damned by the patronizing phrase 'nouveau'.

Ironically, I suppose they are deeply pained by this, moving quickly by Cadillac from one Dallas public-relations agent to another. '*Can't* we get the wedding mentioned in *The New York Times*? *Can't* we have Alexandre flown over from Paris to do our hair before the ball? *Can't* we import a real duchess with lineage and export a rich oil daughter to a masculine European with a title? *Can't* we be ACCEPTED in Paris, LIONIZED in London, WORSHIPPED in Beirut, LOVED in New York, and ENVIED in Houston?'

And I keep on saving my new pennies in old jars. Nouveau pauvre. Old pauvre. Bright new pennies. Enough of them, and one might . . .

2

You made me sweat today. You made me swear. You don't know me personally, yet I know that you know me and that I am somebody to you and can communicate with you.

I watched you from Row P, Seat 6 in convocation today. And then I listened. You don't impress me. You simply give me courage to do what I must. Someone said, 'How can he fit religion into what he said?' I was floored. What you said to me was profoundly and beautifully religious in every sense of the word. What's religion? A way of life, isn't it? *No, no, no – it ISN'T that boxed up package of candy to sweeten your tooth for Sunday*. It is a way of life.

I cry for communication. Where's the student-faculty communication in its real essence? Nowhere. What am I in college for? If I don't learn how to cry out, how to govern myself *here*, how to learn independence within the context of *my own rules*, when do I learn it? We're hidden here – fed, clothed, protected, spoon-fed from the naughty world outside. And oh, poor graduates, why do you *ask* when you are shattered by the 'world outside' *how* it could have happened? Don't our administrators, teachers, those who call themselves our 'guidance dept.,' don't they see how much they're hurting us?

Why must we be bound? I've tasted freedom. Like Baldwin or Paton say in relation to the Negro-white question: It is the white man who is enslaved, not the Negro. So you see, we can't move until we free ourselves, not only in relation to the 'Negro question', but any other question.

Letter from a university student

3

'Don't burn. Soul brother.' A sign on a store window on a ravaged Detroit black slum street, in July, 1967.

Something has *happened* on the street. (Nothing ever

happened before.) Now, whites are here, looking out of their car windows at gutted buildings. (Whites didn't ever come here before.) Now, politicians are arguing on the front pages about who is responsible for the catastrophe. (This place was never on *any* front page before.) Now, it is apparent there has been no communication between black people *here* and so-called Negro leaders downtown, *there*, with the politicians. (Now, the house niggers can't betray the field niggers any more, because the boss man knows there's serious trouble in the fields and he knows he's got to start talking with somebody down there.)

The National Guard, man, are tired, bored, sorry for themselves, and want to go home. Some black women of the slum just brought them hot food from their kitchens

A man stands in front of burned ruins of an apartment house where rats and people had lived. Three youngsters run, laughing, down a street where storefronts are boarded up. Somebody has painted a fresh red-and-blue sign on a store which had 'soul brother' written on its window, so it was not burned.

Life is going on; it is already a minute later.

4

I was asked, in a long-distance telephone call, to be the Protestant speaker during a Religious Emphasis Week at a university. 'We already have our Catholic and our Jew', I was told. I could only reply that I considered myself as Catholic as the Catholic and as Jewish as the Jew, and wondered precisely how one might define Protestant.

In any event, I told the party on the phone, I couldn't imagine why, in this ecumenical age, Jewish students would want to hear yet another Jew, Catholic students yet another Catholic, and Protestant students – supposedly everybody from Mormons to Anglo-Catholics, Christian Scientists to Greek Orthodox – yet another 'Protestant'. (This is education?) I declined.

The next day my phone rang again. The same university was calling. The other speakers had been cancelled. Would I come as the speaker? I said that I would come as myself, not under all sorts of labels, and I did.

5 Summer Day

Where is the shade to let me hide? The sun is an angry god (god is *not* dead, despite the feverish ruminations of some neurotic seminarians; I feel his lash).

I think it would be cool to hide from the angry god. The ten commandments are harsh in the cloudless sky. The creed is a hot stone baking on the dusty ground.

Run! I must run from the angry god who is scorching the earth and burning my bare arms. Damn you, let me go, can't you? What price will you extract from me, after you have drained all strength, all moisture?

A small green leaf on an old tree gives me sanctuary.

6

To a student:

My advice to you is to stir up change, probe for what is the honest factor in anything, help what is new to be born. You must fight the status quo when it is lazy, complacent and indulgent. Be a student! Don't accept anything (God, family, school, sex, love, education, marriage, government) at face value. Ask questions about everything. Dig. Cut through the webs of hypocrisy by always having yet *another* question to ask. If you don't do this, you are failing, not just yourself, but all of us.

7 *He's over Ten:*

Don't trust him.

8 *The Press Is Trigger-Happy*

when it comes to applying the adjective 'controversial' to people. Why doesn't it also make the use of the description 'noncontroversial?' (Example: The Reverend John Jones, noncontroversial Episcopal priest, addressed a gathering on the university campus last night.)

9

The observer – of life, of today, of the moment – must climb up to a vantage point from where he may look down on the human scene. In his vision there is a brisk wind, the sun is blazing, a battle is at a pitch of fury on the plain below. His blood and his fortunes are involved in the fray, yet he stands as one outside this dramatic battle. What does he feel? Is it not an acute loneliness? Does he not wish to be caught up in the intensity and enormity and hotly felt meaning of the battle, even though it may cost him his life? even though he may intellectualize away the depth of the intensity, ridicule the enormity, feel simply frustrated and even hopelessly confused about the meaning of the battle?

He had wanted peace. He knows now that it does not exist, not in the way he had foolishly thought. He would go down into the battle, but he tarries another moment. This non-involvement cuts him like a knife; he bleeds within; his pain is acute. But still he waits, and the moment loses consciousness of time. One must lose one's life if one would save it. He sees this, but hesitates. Besides, there is no joy, no purpose, in the non-involved moment. He wonders: must this moment be for ever? Must this moment be my hell?

From 'If I Go to Hell' by the author

long before my intellect caught up. My intellect kept busy for a long time when my conscience remained conveniently dormant. I did not have to commit myself at all. Then, indignation, intellect, conscience and commitment finally had a head-on collision while I was sitting on a freedom ride bus. We learn more from experience than from anything else. All the thought and moral processes that went into my boarding the freedom ride bus were not nearly so important as just my being on it.

I had now thrown away all roadmaps. I had no idea where I was going, in the next hour or the next five years, but I was damned well committed to the going. It is refreshing to tear down all the assumed security. One can get down to the core of what one's life is all about.

Mine was another body on the bus. It didn't seem so important at that moment whose body it was. It was one of twenty-seven bodies pledged to be there. Meaning took over when strategy did. It matters in the total war if a bridge is captured; it matters in the total war that twenty-seven men got on a bus instead of twenty-three, and that the bus moved along the highway to a particular destination. One wished, sitting on the bus, to say this to the people who have a way of asserting that nothing matters.

11 *At the Flicks:* A Man for All Seasons

Protest costs.

12

I'm writing because of the riots. I'm writing about shootings, lootings, killings, woundings, sorrow, hatred, prejudice – you know what I'm writing about! Sitting here, I'm safe.

I'm comfortable (white, middle-class, college educated, young, well fed – maybe even a bit too well fed), but, *but*, I'm hurting inside.

How did it start? Well, I guess first with Cain and Abel. Or was it in Africa with the importing of the first black man to pick the white man's gold – cotton? Ever since that black man has been emasculated, castrated in fact (the southern lynch mob) and in fiction (the growing lies of prejudice). The black man has not been allowed to be a man.

So now black men mete out their years of hurt, frustration and pain. . . . 'Here's for Selma!' . . . 'There's for the three girls bombed in Birmingham!' . . . 'Here's for Clyde Kennard!' . . . 'There's for the years of lynching, robbing, looting, raping of the "Negro", of the black man.'

He strikes back. How does he do it? He does it with the tool most stamped with the mark 'Made in America' – with good old American violence. They talk about 'Mom's apple pie', but what's more American than cowboys killing Indians? They talk about 'baseball', but what's more American than the 'good' American soldiers killing the 'bad' Communists?

Can he win? Hell no! But is it really a matter of winning? Not really. It's nothing more than a statement, it's the 'Fuck you, Whitey' of the black extremist; it's a man saying 'You know, I don't need you any more to help me get what I deserve. You haven't helped me (why should you, you'd only be cutting out yourself) and so now I'm going it alone. I'm man enough. Man enough!'

Letter from a social worker

13

Going so fast: where, where?
Going so fast: to whom, to whom?

Going so fast: when (what does time mean?), when (what
   does time mean?)?
But why, going so fast? But why, going so fast?

14

The news makes it appear as if there might really be a new
world war today. Helplessly, I read the paper, watch the TV,
and hear the whole thing again over the radio.

Why can't all major egomaniacs realize there are now
simply too many people in the world, and too many weapons
for killing us, to *permit* this?

We're not living in a Hapsburg stage-set kingdom, or in a
romantic, lusty era of knights, armadas and walled cities with
drawbridges. This is now. Damn it, *stop* the bombs!

The war you see on TV may be your last.

15 *A Prayer*

What can we do about war, Jesus?

I mean, when I read history I find there have always been
wars. But now there can't be wars 'always' any more, or there
won't be any people or meaning or life.

Yet what can we do about this, Lord? Little people seem
very insignificant compared to big governments. There is
national face-saving, raw politics and money-making based on
war. There are international balances of power, treaties and
alliances.

Jesus, can we avoid destroying human life and our world?

16

What's wrong with me? And it's not just me – it's all of us –
my friends and their friends and – all of us. I'm a junior in
college, a Presbyterian, with a good solid, white middle-class

background. And I know that life is a drag, it can practically be hell. I want to believe. I do believe but it's hard to trust in and talk to a God that is so vague and out of it all. If he's going to mean anything to me, he's got to understand that despite having 'everything', there's so much missing. Meaning, I guess.

Letter from a university student

17 Thank You, Ladies and Gentlemen!

It is our pleasure again tonight, for the tenth consecutive year, to bring you the award-winning television show, 'What's My Race?' On behalf of my colleagues on the panel, our guest this evening, and our sponsors, Bleach and Tan, we wish you all welcome. Tonight we will bring you a documentary programme in celebration of our tenth anniversary on television. But first, I have a brief word from our sponsors, Bleach and Tan. Are you self-conscious about being too light or too dark? Would you like to try new skin tints or shades, to vary your whole personality make-up, make new friends and bring out hitherto unknown facets about you? Now you can feel *free*, now you can change the *old* you into the *new* you you have dreamed about. Did you dream about it in black and white? Now you can make your dreams come true in Technicolor. Now you can be as stark white or jet black, as rosy-cream or golden-brown, as you have secretly always wished to be. Liberate your secret dreams. If you feel washed-out and pale, *think* colour, *feel* colour, *be* colourful. If you feel more colourful than you want to be, *think* white, *feel* white, *be* white. Use Bleach *or* Tan ... get *both* in the giant economy package. Get integrated ... today. And remember our other great products, Magnolia chewing-gum and Magnolia, the wisteria deodorant. Visit our factory and showrooms on *your* family vacation, in Albany, Georgia. You will always receive a warm welcome.

Bring the whole family. And stay for lunch, dinner, or a sit-in, in the Magnolia Tearoom.

From 'The Job', an unpublished play by the author

18 *What Does "Sexy" Mean*

Does it mean itching to have sex all the time, having it, or appearing to have it?

I mean, does 'sexy' rightly pertain to the archetypal unmarried librarian who hasn't had sexual relations with any man since her ill-fated love affair forty years ago, and thinks about sex constantly? *Is* sex the itch itself?

Or, take that plain, rather unattractive, certainly unglamorous looking couple over there. Nobody would seriously think about having sex with either of them. But they have sex relations almost daily, and after a decade of marriage, remain erotic athletes. Are they sexy? (But this could mean the demise of images.)

Look at the sex goddess. She hasn't had a satisfactory sex relationship since her stepfather tried to molest her as a child, yet she is a real presence in the dreams of millions of men. Her smile, the way she speaks, but mostly her walk: These are known in far away jungles and deserts and great cities as the epitome of sex. Is she sexy?

Is the definitive answer to the question to be found in a Hollywood movie studio, the English court, the Paris follies, an Egyptian belly-dancing school, Vassar, a New York advertising agency, a university in Stockholm, a Sicilian village, high society in Rio de Janeiro, the aristocracy of New Delhi, an office in Ghana, or a little-theatre project in Indianapolis?

19 *The Radio*

What time will the next news go on? I haven't heard news for a half hour. I don't want to be *alone*. If the news comes on again in a few minutes, I won't be alone. I think the 6 P.M. newscaster is very sincere, don't you? He seems to be so, well, you know, real. You get a feeling you can believe in him. With the news on, you're not alone.

20 War Games

Whatever the explanation one can see that the U.S. planes are dropping the enormous weight of explosives on purely civilian targets. It is the civilians who have taken the punishment. President Johnson's announced policy that American targets in Vietnam are steel and concrete rather than human lives seems to have little connection with the reality of attacks carried out by U.S. planes.

Harrison Salisbury, in the 'New York Times'

Nothing could have prepared me for my encounters with Vietnamese women and children burned by napalm. ... It was shocking and sickening for me as a physician to see and smell the blackened flesh. ... one can never forget the bewildered eyes of the silent suffering napalm-burned children.

Dr R. E. Perry, in 'Redbook'

I have also seen a napalm victim. This man had caught the full ferocity of the napalm bomb's fire. His body had been awash with the stuff. From his scalp to the soles of his feet, his skin was peeling as if from an obscene suntan. Yet he survived. That is, perhaps, the most horrible thing about napalm and white phosphorus: though the body is virtually drowned in flame, the victim tends to live.

Anthony Carthew, in the London 'Sun'

Okay.

It's about the complacency, the laziness, the withdrawal.

Do you know that I don't even listen to or read the news every day? How hard it is to communicate with people who aren't on my wavelength without giving up the effort to really talk with them, to maintain that delicate balance? How I so often can't stand to be with people who are on my wavelength for very long?

I don't seem to be capable of a sustained effort. And I must try to study, not to wallow in my hang-ups, and yet not to fear involvement?

Should I rewrite this goddamn letter, so it will be at least more intelligible?

How can I live, and do something besides just feel responsive to so many things. It's an effort to be aware of and relate to the people around me. But at the same time I should be aware of things and people not immediately around me, concentrating on *something* besides term papers, friends who are 'snowed', and our emotional stability. (Why so preoccupied with fear of going mad, 'cracking up'? I suspect – I know – that I'm not quite that delicate, and can take a hell of a lot more of emotional jostling than I am now.)

How do you get mature in a hurry?

Letter from a university student

22

A man may be of value to another man, not because he wishes to be important, not because he possesses some inner wealth of soul, not because of something he is, but because of what he is – not. His importance may consist in his poverty, in his hopes and fears, in his waiting and hurrying, in the direction of his whole being towards what lies beyond his horizon and beyond his power. The importance of an apostle is negative rather than positive. In him a void becomes visible. And for this reason he is something to others: he is able to share grace with them, to focus their attention, and to establish them in waiting and in adoration. The Spirit gives grace through him.

From 'The Epistle to the Romans' by Karl Barth

23

It can be argued that a great deal ought not to be expected of the church. It is certainly theologically correct to acknowledge that, institutionally, it is ridden with the same moral ambiguities as General Motors, S.N.C.C., the State Department, the Teamsters' Union, the University of Michigan, the A.M.A. or the U.S. Marines. Yet granting this, one must still expect more of the church precisely because of its own claims that more should be expected.

From 'A Plea to Laymen to Jolt Christianity,' by the author, in 'The Wall Street Journal'

24

There was a handful of Negro students in a prestigious, middle-sized liberal arts college where I was visiting. I sat up, through most of a night, talking with the dozen Negroes who were sprinkled through the 1400-member student body. 'I don't want to hate whites,' one girl said. 'I try not to. But when I'm with them, I can't help it.'

Another student explained how she felt it was an iron necessity always to wear a mask and play a role when she was with white persons.

One student in the group had recently stood up in a school meeting and addressed the assembled whites: 'I am not the same as you. I don't want to be the same as you. I am black and you are white. You must understand this. In order to treat me as a human being, you must be able to see me as a human being who is black.'

25

What we need to discover in the social realm is the moral equivalent of war: something heroic that will speak to men as universally as war does, and yet will be as compatible with their spiritual selves as war has proved itself to be incompatible. I have often thought that in the old monkish poverty-worship ... there might be something like that moral equivalent of war which we are seeking. Might not voluntarily accepted poverty be 'the strenuous life', without the need of crushing weaker peoples? ...

Among us English-speaking peoples especially do the praises of (voluntary) poverty need once more to be boldly sung. We have grown literally afraid to be poor. We despise anyone who elects to be poor in order to simplify and save his inner life. If he does not join the general scramble and pant with the money-making street, we deem him spiritless and lacking in ambition. ...

Think of the strength which personal indifference to poverty would give us if we were devoted to unpopular causes. We need no longer hold our tongues or fear to vote the revolutionary or reformatory ticket. Our stocks might fall, our hopes of promotion vanish, our salaries stop, our club doors close in our faces; yet, while we lived, we would imperturbably bear witness to the spirit, and our example would help to set free our generation. ...

I recommend this matter to your serious consideration.

From 'The Varieties of Religious Experience' by William James

26

The sun at the end of the street is blinding this morning. Its heat burns me through the closed window. The window is blazing. This, without tongues of fire or flashing, piercing lights on the street outside. Its light is constant, turning it to silver.

The sun's rays ricochet off the walls of the house next door. It is shining through trees and buildings and people. The path leading towards it moves in a clean line, *straight, straight* up the street, towards the corner.

I would like to follow it.

27

So we found it necessary to examine the emotional associations people had with kippers. We found that kippers have a very foreign sound to most people. They visualize poor people in foreign countries who can't afford anything better, and minority groups in their own country. They think of dirty docks and foreigners with smelly boats. Most of their associations with kippers are both strange and unappetizing. What we found is that kippers are in a sense an un-American food. It's not what the good, middle-class housewife can safely serve to her friends. The advertising problem, therefore, was not to prove that kippers taste delicious. The problem was to Americanize kippers, to tie it in with accepted American foods, to make it familiar, to show how to use it, to show it against average, middle-class backgrounds in ordinary situations . . . to make it a perfectly safe, average, secure thing to serve.

From 'What Makes People Do Things?' address delivered by Dr. Virginia Miles, an expert in motivation research in the advertising field, before the Grocery Manufacturers of America; quoted in 'Crisis in Communication' by the author

28

Those whites who are really committed to civil rights can make it clear to society at large that a significant minority of Americans will no longer accept equivocation and procrastination. But it is far easier to deal with racial problems by writing letters to congressmen than to demonstrate one's own freedom. Every individual who rises above the constrictions of race is a demonstration that this is really possible. Every time a Negro sees a group of secretaries – white and Negro – chatting over lunch; or children – white and Negro – walking together to school, he feels that hope is possible. Every time his white friend shows he is not afraid to argue with him as with anyone else, he sees that freedom is possible, that there are some for whom race is irrelevant, who accept or reject a person not as a Negro or a white, but in terms of himself. Only so can the real confinements of the ghetto be broken. The Negro cannot win alone this fight that transcends the 'civil rights struggle'. White and Negro must fight together for the rights of human beings to make mistakes and to aspire to human goals. Negroes will not break out of the barriers of the ghetto unless whites transcend the barriers of their own minds, for the ghetto is to the Negro a reflection of the ghetto in which the white lives imprisoned. The poetic irony of American race relations is that the rejected Negro must somehow also find the strength to free the privileged white.

From 'The Dark Ghetto' by Kenneth B. Clark

29

How do you think parents should react when they find out their son or daughter has had a sex relation?

Letter from a high-school student

When the man came back from his son's grave, he told me he had wanted to pray but could not, for he didn't know the words of any prayers. I was sad that he did not realize he was praying just by standing there.

31

A teacher in a slum school asked the class: 'Who are we, what are we doing here, and where are we going?'

A girl in the class smiled noncommittally, waiting for the answer.

SEPTEMBER

1

It is not yet morning. I am in intolerable pain, which cannot be eased. But I am waiting for the first hint of light. It will be comforting, provide a break, somehow represent an actual release.

There *is* mystery in living and dying. Great, great pain (and its reminder of the certainty of death) renders so fragile proud reliance on practicality and iron self-sufficiency. It is just that we have needs which we do not know how to meet.

I think, then, that knowing about mystery is very beautiful. There are vistas that exist without our seeing them.

2 *The Church Is Caught in a Real Revolution*

For years there was a misunderstanding that God had nothing to do with politics or the arts, economics or sociology, but that he was the God of the holy hour in an expensive building, locked up most of the time. Now this notion has been knocked, quite effectively, on the head. It was a terrible heresy – that archaic word! – to remove God from life. An old, old friend said to me: 'When my wife and I are engaged in the sexual act, God turns his back.' And I could only reply: 'What an awful thing to say about your wife, the sexual act and God.' But he is so pathetically typical. People pay a little pledge. They go home from their lone hour in the church building, get out of their good clothes, turn on TV, start acting natural, and believe that this is their life without God.

3

I had a daydream one day that Christ returned 'unobtrusively' and I said I know that's Christ, but underneath I doubted.

He said 'follow me' and I did but we never stopped to eat or drink, and I died along the way because I didn't have enough faith in him. 'Oh ye of little faith.' This sentence hits me hard and the wound just never heals.

Don't tell me, please, that this is a bunch of shit because it's *not*. Honestly, it's not.

Letter from a university student

4

Let's not get into identities. Please, just let me be functional.

5

One of my ex-friends is very impressed with herself and considers herself quite a 'good Christian'. But when she found out that a boy named Don plays his guitar at the coffeehouse, that he is a Negro, and that I consider him a friend, she really went through the floor. (Wait till my mother hears that I hang around with coloured kids!) I asked her if she had ever met a Negro, hating myself for having to come to her level in a 'those people' sense. She said that there had been a 'good one' in her fourth-grade class, but that of course she didn't want to get 'involved'. 'Why don't you come down and meet Don next Saturday?' 'I've got better things to do.' Finally, exasperated, I said, 'Don't worry; I see a lot of nice little white boys, too.' Of course, that didn't solve anything.

I really don't know what to say. God, what am I supposed to say? When someone calls me a 'dirty Jew', I can just ignore him. But this person doesn't even know Don, what a wonderful person he is. All she pretends to know is his colour.

Basically, I don't have the courage of my convictions; I'm afraid to speak my mind. At school, kids ask me why I'm so funny, why I care about civil rights and the war in Vietnam, and I want acceptance, so I deny my involvement. Then afterwards I feel lousy, and I think about the kids I worked with in Head Start, and I realize that every time I deny my involvement, I'm hurting them, pushing them back into their ghetto. What am I supposed to do? What should I do? I want to get out and really help someone, but I'm selfish and afraid. I can't go on just singing those darned freedom songs forever.

Letter from a university student

6

I am an invisible man. No, I am not a spook like those who haunted Edgar Allan Poe; nor am I one of your H-film ectoplasms. I am a man of substance, of flesh and bone, fibre and liquids – and I might even be said to possess a mind. I am invisible, understand, simply because people refuse to see me. Like the bodiless heads you see sometimes in circus sideshows, it is as though I have been surrounded by mirrors of hard, distorting glass. When they approach me they see only my surroundings, themselves, or figments of their imagination – indeed, everything and anything except me.

From 'Invisible Man' by Ralph Ellison

7 *The Glamour of Travel*

Vast, cavernous hotels. Stone shafts outside dreary windows. Thermostat-controlled air, not quite human, not hot, not cold. Going up and down – again and again and again – in lifts that play constant tinny music. A cellophane cover over the drinking glass in the bathroom – this is provided *every day* so that one can't even get used to drinking out of the same glass for three or four days.

While recuperating from such a glamorous trip, one hears somebody say, 'I wish *I* could take a trip.' That green grass again, on the other side of the road.

8 *At the Flicks:* The War Game

This is the way it happens.

9

I went round the mound of earth and stood before the gigantic grave. People lay in it so closely packed one upon the other that only their heads could be seen. The trench was already three-quarters full. By my reckoning there were already about a thousand people lying in it. I looked round to see who was shooting. An SS man sat at the edge of the trench letting his legs dangle in it; he had a submachine gun resting on his knee and was smoking a cigarette.

The completely naked people went down a few steps which had been dug in the wall of the trench, scrambled over the heads of those who were lying there to the position that the SS man indicated. They lay down among the dead or wounded people; some stroked those who were still alive, and spoke quietly to them. Then I heard a succession of shots. I looked in the trench and saw how the bodies twitched; blood spurted from the necks. I was surprised that no one told me to go away, but I also saw two or three postmen in uniform standing near by.

From sworn testimony by the German engineer, Herman Friedrich Grabe, in 'The Nuremburg Trial'

10 *Late-Night Blues in the City*

Looking at it from my window in the middle of the night, it consists of stone shafts speckled with lights, reaching high into the sky, and labyrinthine streets and alleys far, far below, some illuminated by a flood or touch of light, others hidden in shadows.

It is all very romantic, and very deceptive. For the pretty picture doesn't show the people who, at this moment, aren't in the picture at all. It doesn't show the waste in human life and energy, the tragedies in city planning, the squalid discomfort, the extremes between haves and have-nots, the industrial fumes and car exhaust, the overcrowded schools which long ago ceased to educate students and now are only factories on shifts, and the crime which grows when there is no longer hope but simply frustration and despair.

I am a child and a man of the city. Its sickness, or its health, is mine. So does my sickness, or health, contribute to its own. We must find a way to get well together.

11 *To a Boy on a Bicycle*

Wearing your bright-red sweater, riding far down the street underneath lush green trees heavy with leaves, you seem to be a figure in a poetic documentary film.

This view of you is romantic and misleading, though you don't yet know it. Life for you is somewhat lonely, but there are many compensations. You are rich, the sole heir to a great fortune. You generally eat in front of the TV set with a butler. This, of course, is because your family is more often than not out for the evening.

Your grades aren't very good, but you'll be sent to the best prep school money and solid family influence can buy. Later, you'll end up at a socially acceptable college where less-than-brilliant rich kids seem to congregate.

But then what? It could be a lot of different things, if you only understood that you are free. Maybe there's less mobility in your social and economic class than in any other. You want to please your parents and do what they expect of you.

But there's a world out there, a new world, ripe for the taking. A boy of your age in a slum may ultimately have more freedom to be a person than you, for he may at least have radically different alternatives open to him.

You're riding on your bicycle over to the country club for a swim.

12

I can understand the ratmaze feeling you have described, and sympathize. On the other hand, I expect that if the dynamic imperative *were* in the place and the situation, one would not be aware of it till afterwards. (Jacob said *afterwards* 'surely the Lord was in this place, and I knew it not'), so perhaps it is, and we are not meant to know it.

Letter from a friend who teaches philosophy at a university

13

I worry about God all the time. I think I mostly believe in him, or force myself to believe in him, out of desperation. I can't make it without faith in something, so I use God as my crutch. Once in a while I have genuine faith in and love for him, but not very often. What's the point? And vague as he is to me, why do I always want to regain my faith, why do I feel I can't live without it? (Although my real life consists of three and a half hours every Saturday night.)

Letter from a university student

14 *Can the Church Act As Reconciler in Society?*

It is not difficult to rationalize away the sharp meaning of 'reconciler'. It can be perverted to mean soft compromiser, meek agent of acquiescence in social evils, gently sentimental moderate, or apostate symbol of the status quo whose final allegiance is to society instead of God.

The church can act as reconciler by scrupulously looking to the breakdowns in its own moral and intellectual integrity, listening before it speaks, not being afraid to speak at whatever human cost when it knows it must, and, at the core of everything, struggling to continue loving. The church may hate a sin but it must love the sinner. Its heady egoism, titillated by the possession of spiritual power, must be sacrificed. The church, being prepared to die for the sake of God because it worships God and not itself, must love others enough to be humble before them.

Knowing its true identity, the church need not rely on human success symbols but should always remember the desperate need others may have of such symbols, and consequently show mercy and understanding to such men. The church is meant to be a servant in society, serving God by serving men. Remembering the marks of its vocation, the church can call itself, again and again, back to the crucial business of loving. When it loves it is the reconciler.

15

BAN GIN
or
Legalize Pot

a man in funny robes says some traditional words over the two of us in a strange building, does that make it right, and if he doesn't, does that mean it's wrong?

Letter from a woman student in a university

17

To a Young Man Who Plans to Be a Clergyman.

Nancy startled me, I must confess, when she told me that you intend, once you get out of prison, to study to become a clergyman. I wonder how you see this role?

I can't see you inside a church building on Sunday morning at 11 o'clock, officiating in the tight, formal service, mounting a tall pulpit to preach a sermon. On the other hand, I can see you functioning quite easily as an ordained man in the Underground Church.

For that you would need secular employment to use your skills and provide your income. (You should decide now what these skills are and what fresh education you need to implement them.) This ministry would bring you very, very close to people – people in their natural work and life, not behind the façade of the 'holy hour' on Sunday morning.

Have you read some of the 'God is Dead' theology? It is one of the few signs of life in Christian theology in a long time. And, of course, God *is* dead, if, indeed, God ever lived: the God of our fantasies, worship, Establishment and utility. The God of 'In God We Trust'. The tribal 'God' who loved our nation and hated our enemies in war, won track meets and football games for Christian athletes, cured head colds on cue, and even got a girl into Kappa Kappa Gamma *if* she prayed hard enough. The transcendent, American, white God is cold, cold dead in the market. Proclaim it! Meanwhile, — —is not dead.

No one can honestly tell you what the church will be in five, ten, or twenty years from now. But I imagine you will find underground churches in communities and as communities. The underground's passionate concern for church unity will be expressed increasingly in action of unity itself. Along with this, there will continue to be a sense of radical (not liberal) participation in social action. Your prison term is, therefore, very much of an underground witness. You are in prison because of your opposition to war and refusal to serve the military. Don't forget, this is alien, queer and 'evil' to many, many Americans. Your action, which must remain unintelligible to the Establishment (or else be construed as a kind of treason), is understood within the underground. I'm sure you see the underground for what it is – not a 'new' church but simply a centre for community and service.

What I see of the present Underground Church reveals an almost desperate fear of acquiring the kind of power which corrupts men and their institutions. Yet there must be power to meet power. This is, and apparently will continue to be, a dilemma of the underground. It realizes that there is power in ideas and convictions – especially in an age of mass communications – as much as in buildings, prestige, traditions and bank accounts.

Your ministry, hopefully, will be a style of life instead of a carbon copy of prescribed forms along with ghettoization from other people's real lives. Piety should not be separated from any other part of your life but rather be a part of the whole – discipleship of Jesus. So there won't be a part of you which is *clergyman* and another which is *man*! You are simply yourself, and studied bits of role-playing in 'separated' situations of life must be non-existent in the wholeness of your humanity.

18 Condemnation

Listen to me, o brothers,
Six Vietcong were here in my village yesterday
My birthplace was bombarded and completely destroyed!
Nobody survives
Only foundations of houses are seen
With the burned bamboo bushes
And a destroyed pagoda without roof and altar
I am back here today, contemplating cloud and river.

In the presence of tonight's stars,
In the presence of all mankind on this earth,
In the presence of you, o my fellow men,
Let me raise my voice to condemn this savage war of brothers.
Let me ask: who has pushed us into this murderous quicksand?
Be the witness tonight
And listen to me
I do not accept this way
I never have and I never will.
I want to repeat this a thousand times before they kill me
Listen to me as to a Do Quyen, dropping blood from its beak
    and crying out until death, for the sake of its mate,
Turn your arms to fight hatred
Our enemy is fanaticism, violence, it's cupidity, it's calumny,
Our enemy is not man – even man bearing the label 'Viet-
    cong'
If we kill man, with whom shall we live?

A poem by Thich Nhat Hanh, monk and member of the Fellowship of Reconciliation

19 For Richer, for Poorer

At first they were lovers. Then they became man and wife.
One day they realized they had also become friends. For nearly
forty years they've been living together. Their marriage has

become synonymous with their friendship. They are grateful because it has remained, especially under stresses and strains, something that always keeps growing.

20

My brother in Bratislava, Czechoslovakia, is riding to work on his motorcycle at 6:30 A.M., his lunch in a brown paper bag. My brother in Pittsburgh is riding to work in his car at 6:30 A.M., his lunch in a brown paper bag.

How can they meet as brothers?

21 *The Film and I*

It is being projected on to a screen at the other end of the long room. Images are moving. I hear words and music. All of us sitting here in this room are very silent, absorbed.

Is *that* reality or fantasy? It seems to me somehow more real than my own life. Realism is this film's style, humanness its content. Yet it is a film. The actors are actors; they do not live in the poor hovels I see on the screen, but in grand houses and great hotels. They are not hungry and emaciated as they now appear. The terrible dilemmas of the persons are scripted; the actors can check out at 5 P.M., have the make-up and costumes removed, and drive home for a drink before dinner.

Yet I am absorbed in what seems real. Of course, it is real for the characters who are portrayed. But have they a life? If so, what is the relation between their lives, under greasepaint, to mine without it?

A few minutes ago I was laughing out loud at something very funny up there. Now I am sitting in stony silence, un-aware whether my own heart is beating, closer to tears than I am aware (indeed, they may be brought over the brink by the right use of music, or a clever use of the camera *if* it moves, right now, from the exterior snow scene through that window into the living room where a father and his son confront one another).

Images. Sounds. Lights. Greasepaint.

Soon I will be outside the theatre, walking on the street. Will the only reality then be inside myself, or will I have returned to fantasy from the reality on the screen?

22 *He's No Longer One of the Church Big Shots*

That was just a phase, when he was new at the game of being an Important Layman. It was flattering to have lunch with a bishop or a dean, be sought after by the church's public relations experts, and attend hand-picked conferences on 'Laymen's Work' in New York, Chicago and San Francisco.

He even became a vestryman in the top Power Structure (his term, in this instance) parish of the diocese. Everyone knew he had the bishop's ear, so he was treated with deference to his face, and with churlish envy behind his back.

He was never rock-solid in his profession *or* in Society. That is to say, he had worked for, instead of inheriting, what he owned; so he could never be considered 'old family'. In his church, that was always held against him. One's *blood* always told, it was quietly but decisively said.

Enough essential Christianity rubbed off on him so that, when the race and peace issues started crackling locally, he took a stance in line with his convictions. This made him a maverick on the vestry and in the diocesan councils. Other issues and similar stands followed.

Cocktail party invitations dwindled sharply. So did his law practice. His name disappeared gradually from church boards and other prestigious places.

He has a better sense now of who he is and what he can hope to achieve. He hasn't fled the Power Structure, but remains inside, speaking his mind, needling, working out strategies within the community. He is no longer alone; unexpected allies have turned up. He believes one best talks about God when he speaks about what is human. So his focus has shifted from *that* world to *this* one, from 'religion' to, well, life.

23

Night voices have left the dark street below and come into my room.

They are strangers, but not unwelcome. Yet I cannot identify them. One is shrill (no, I suppose really it's not; this is only its guise). Another is almost hysterically happy (I wonder, will it be so in the morning?). Evidently the voices belong to people returning home late from a party.

Now, the particular voices in this particular street have quickly become silenced. The people have gone. The voices are dead, absent or still. How odd, the vacuum in which there are no voices.

24

How can I be a witness for Christ when I can only witness to the experience of others? I *believe*, but it's all in my *head*. There is no actuality of experience. This makes me so envious and resentful. I'm trapped in *myself*.

Letter from a housewife

25 *From a Primer for Gentleman:*

Wrestle, if you must, but with *very correct* ghosts.

26

In a place like this where so many are lonely, it would be inexcusably selfish to be lonely alone.

From 'Camino Real' by Tennessee Williams

27 A Prayer

The jazz is good, Jesus, but all the people here tonight seem so damned lonely.

We're somehow separated from each other and can only feign communication by stupid smiles or even more meaningless small-talk. So most of us gave up trying to communicate (whatever that really means) some time ago.

Now it's just the jazz and the drinks. The jazz is digging in. It's saying a lot of things, and these have somehow started binding us together.

Will we be a kind of community here tonight, Lord? I suppose we already are and don't know it. But, Jesus, what about tomorrow? Will anything be left or will it all be smashed into very separate pieces?

Help us, Jesus, to hold on to whatever we've got going here in the way of community, will you? At least help us to hold on to some kind of relationship with each other and you.

28

They had to let Thelma, their coloured maid, go. She was completely irresponsible. No, not in her work, but she was just like a child, you know, and then they found she was keeping a bottle of gin under her bed. Well, naturally, they got her out of there like a bolt of lightning. I guess Art just bundled her up right on the spot and dropped her at a bus stop with her things. I understand Thelma was crying when Art left her at the bus stop. You just don't know what to do with people like that. Well, they don't have our advantages, for one thing. And they're *different*. That's all you can say about it. They're *different*.

29

Have confidence, Majesty, God is white. . . . For two thousand years God has been white. He eats on a white table cloth. He wipes his white mouth with a white napkin. He picks at white meat with a white fork. (*A Pause*). He watches the snow fall.

From 'The Blacks' by Jean Genet

30

Memo from a press agent to the producer of a biblical spectacular film:

Last night, when I saw the rushes, I wondered about the orgy scene. Could you possibly underplay it more? Remember, the N. Y. critics lambasted you for the same thing the last time. Couldn't you make a concession to them without losing dough in Indianapolis?

I suggest, in line with your new image we talked about over lunch Tuesday, that you join a panel of biblical scholars for, say, an eight-minute segment of a new TV documentary. (This will NOT, repeat, NOT be ad lib. I will brief you carefully.) The association with the biblical scholars will lend you dignity and solid weight.

The producers of the TV documentary are especially interested in the research you've done for the new biblical spectacular film. The TV staff wants to make use of the seventy wigs of Esther you had made in Kansas City, the eighty robes of Potiphar's wife you had done in Paris, and the thousand spears you ordered from Beirut for the desert army.

I know you don't care about the kook religious magazines. However, they do reach the Religious Influentials. It just might mean dough this time if they liked the picture. *Christian Century* and *Commonweal* hit you pretty hard last time on the twenty-minute rape scene in the temple. They used as a gimmick the fact that it isn't in the Bible. Maybe you could somehow be more subtle with the sex this time. Do you hear me? If I'm out of line, please forgive me, but I feel I should raise these issues now.

There may be a national magazine cover story on the 120 elephants you got for the battle scene. Especially if you can provide some of the girl extras to pose with them. Maybe, for one shot, a girl extra could be chained and we could get a picture of an elephant about to crush her. If I couldn't sell this to a national mag, I could get a hot wirephoto on it. It's got sex, animals, danger and a built-in plug.

As you know, some of the reviewers have got downright nasty about your biblical spectaculars. *Life* did a mean piece the last time, *McCall's* got the hatchet out, and *Esquire* – sorry, I didn't mean to bring that up again. But all this supports an idea I've got.

Invite the snottiest reviewers of them all – yes, sir – invite them straight out. NOT to a week in Las Vegas. NOT to Hawaii. NOT to an expensive junket in Hollywood or N. Y. But get an out-of-the-way monastery (in Wyoming? Utah?) to cooperate. You know, promise to build them a chapel or something, and explain to them how you're doing God's work.

This is a *million dollar idea*. They'd have to get up early in the morning to attend all the religious services. Eat the monastery food. Do you realize that after all that, they couldn't ever attack your sincerity again? You and the prior (I believe that's the term; all this can be researched and checked out) of the monastery could hold a joint press conference. I can just see all the space you'd get. And IN DEPTH.

P.S. The Interfaith Council is giving you a plaque tomorrow at lunch. It'll be in the Sistine Room (that's the new name we just gave the old Lobster Room in the commissary). Don't smoke. Watch your language. Don't take a drink before lunch. And I'll get you a copy before 10 A.M. of the ancient Hittite grace you're to say just before the group sits down to eat.

All for now. God bless.

OCTOBER

I

May I be quite honest with you? We both know your life is masked, and there is a terrible split within it. One part of you wants a different life, while another part refuses to change. So you exist on a see-saw.

I know there is a key, somewhere, to the puzzle of you. I have not been able to find it, which is my own shortsightedness and failure. If you could only venture forth from the deep recesses in which that frantic, frightened child dwells, and crouch in a safe place to watch the dawn. I have seen, in your eyes, the child. The child is emaciated, hungry, longing, and very pale for a lack of sun. Liberate the child who wants to become an adult.

Liberation is not 'easy'. It takes a single moment of dying. The child wants to be liberated (I know this). The child must either try to become free, or it must ask – cry out – for help.

What you must do is draw closer to others. Healing occurs when it is least sought or anticipated. It occurs, in fact, when one has forgotten about being healed, and has simply entered into the human condition more fully to be with others, and, if possible, serve them.

No matter how tight the mask you place on your face, you can't hide the child's eyes.

2

A small Negro boy came regularly to his play therapy sessions. Each week he entered the playroom, sat at the table, propped back his chair, placed his feet upon the table, and then folded his arms majestically over his chest. Week after week, the child came to the playroom, repeated the performance, and sat with an impassive expression on his face until the session ended. Finally, he asked the therapist if she knew what he had been playing. Eagerly, she confessed that she had no idea. 'I've been playing white man!' he announced.

From 'Play Therapy Procedures and Results' by Virginia M. Axline

3

I am one of those confused teen-agers: I guess sort of a cross between Franny Glass and Holden Caulfield.

I'm Jewish and most of the Christians who I know who are at all religious are always trying to convert me. So I sort of got the impression that most Christians, except those working in poverty and the peace movement, etc., were just concerned about petty sins all the time, and heaven and hell and things like that.

God must really be laughing at us while we argue about such stupid things as whether or not to keep kosher or eat meat on Fridays, or whether or not the Jews really killed Jesus. I mean, I don't think God really cares. There are so many important things going on. I really feel crazy writing to you like this. Like, I've never even met you. But I haven't talked to anyone in so long. I've just got to do something.

P.S. Do you know mrs. mouse or the pituitary dwarf?

Letter from a high-school student

4

Long Beach, California (Associated Press):
Mrs. Virginia Smith delivered her own baby without help while watching television from a couch in her living room.

'It was a good film and I didn't want to turn it off,' Mrs. Smith, thirty-eight years old, explained yesterday.

Mrs Smith's husband, James, a carpenter, had gone to bed in

the next room three hours earlier. She roused him in time to help her snip the umbilical cord with a pair of sewing scissors.

What film *was* it?

5 *I Hadn't Seen Him in a Year*

He's a gifted, celebrated and powerful man. He had someone telephone me to set the time for our meeting. But then, to my dismay, I realized it was to take place in a small crowd. He is never alone now. He no longer stops, even for a moment, to be quiet, or think, or talk with *a person*: He's always rapidly, nervously on the move; and with (that sad, awful word) an entourage.

I wondered, how long could he continue in this way until he suffered a breakdown?

We talked, amid the crowd. Hangers-on and sycophants were everywhere (he pays the bills); they hung intently on his less bright words as if they were brilliant; laughed loudly at his funny and unfunny stories; moved in with conversational thrusts (as they were supposed to do) when he appeared to be momentarily depressed or simply tired.

It was like an *old* royal court. The power play was the cement holding everybody together. Oh, there could be light moments – after all, (*laughs*), we're all human, aren't we? But it takes heavy cash and gruelling labour to keep a personal empire moving. He's essentially simple, and vulnerable and looking for love and joy. When, and why, did he cut away the ground from under him?

6

I work in a very old, conservative business firm which is more than one hundred years old but hired its first Negro 'white-collar man' six months ago. I am white and am his secretary. So I have witnessed his 'stoning'.

The kind of stones that cut and scar more than any rock. To see him at his desk while five men leave the office 'forgetting' to ask him to join them for lunch. To attend an office party and see his beautiful wife 'overlooked' as a dancing partner.

He talks about leaving and returning to the security of the black ghetto, but even there he has already been rejected as a square for playing Whitey's game. He's a bridge, lonely but important.

Letter from an office secretary

7

Some whites think that to teach Negro history in the United States is to teach hatred of whites.

Exactly what parts of Negro history in America would they like to excise? The accounts of *which* slave ships, plantation conditions, lynchings, house burnings, rapes, vote stealing.

What exactly threatens these whites? Do they want to appoint a committee to censor or rewrite our past. It seems to me the best thing is to face it, as history, and make sure the same things never happen again – starting now.

8

When I march in a rally (and I haven't marched in very many), I feel that it's really not getting any of us anywhere. Maybe that's why I haven't been in more. But maybe I'm looking for too big a result. Just being there must give others courage to fight, too – is that it? I don't know. I'm afraid I despair too easily to be a real crusader. There must be something more I – we all – can do. But what?

Letter from a university instructor

9 *Life*

Many an American said
We have to kill for another year in order to have peace,
In order to have peace, do you hear that, younger brother?
One year, or two years, or ten years,
I don't mind
If this boy dies, we still have another.
Smaller boys will grow up, in time.
More guns, more bullets, more boys,
O people who never fear hunger and death
Come, to be our advisers
and to help us to kill us.

This poem, by Thai Luan, a Vietnamese Buddhist, is distributed by the Fellowship of Reconciliation

10 *At the Flicks:* The Shop on Main Street

'What can I do? I'm nobody,' he cried. But he could have done something – and now it was too late.

11 *Are You Bombing with Me, Jesus?*

Poster carried in a peace demonstration in San Francisco in the spring of 1967.

12

There must be mechanics of dying.

One dies. Granted. But how? Is it so simple that one's eyes are open one moment, closed (for ever) the next? This seems absurd. Does a flame go out? 'The heart stops'; it sounds so unromantic. One is warm before and cold afterwards; then apply more blankets, start a fire in the grate, *do something*. The laughter dies. The sweat dries. The passion ceases to be.

Must there be a funeral for me? With people dressed in blacks and greys, women wearing hats, nobody speaking out loud, everyone avoiding any sign of humour or gaiety. An organist playing lugubrious music – abstract, sad things without a definite melody, then, suddenly, a couple of tear-jerker hymns. Then everybody crying.

A sombre clergyman emerges from the wings. The strait-laced, wrung-dry, absolutely morbid service commences. The readings and prayers just make everybody feel worse, because of the associations these things have with funerals in the past. Resurrection from the dead, indeed. This is pure Greek tragedy.

I know a ritual meets needs of 'those remaining'. I'll grant this. But can't the ritual be warm, human, carried out with taste and, yes, beauty? I want people I love to be *involved* in it. I want a folk song in place of an archaic hymn. I want a gathering of friends: Why can't people say what they feel like saying, about the community in which we have all lived, the funeral itself, me, themselves, whatever comes to mind? I should prefer prayers *without* old English. Obviously, there will be no 'eulogy' – if there were, old friends would simply break up laughing, I hope, for it would be vulgar beyond words and Super Press Agentry.

Then, afterwards, I should like everyone to gather in someone's home for a drink, some hot (not cold) food, some talking and some being, maybe laughing about good remembrances. That's it. It's really simple enough.

13

'Hold it, fellows. I just thought of something.' All of the men had stopped now, were standing up straight, listening. Bradshaw lay groaning softly at their feet. 'You fellows know this is our last nigger? Just think on that. Our last nigger, ever. There won't be no more after this, and no more singing and dancing and laughing. The only niggers we'll ever see, unless we go over into Mississippi or Alabama, will be on television and they don't sing none of the old songs, or do the old dances no more. They's high-class niggers with white wives and big cars. I been thinking that while we still got one, we ought to get him to do one of the old songs for us.'

From 'A Different Drummer' by William Melvin Kelley

14 'America':

will it mean Freedom or Fourth Reich?

15 Yom Kippur

Atonement – holiness in the midst of life, confession of sin. *Repentance* – sorrow, a desire for amendment of life, a wish that a heart of stone may become once again a heart of flesh. Creative, deeply rooted action of wholehearted *reconciliation* with God.

16

I remember two of my schoolteachers.

In junior high, there was a history teacher who taught me to love history; it came alive for me, living and breathing. Of course, at the same time, life – and my part in it – opened up too.

In high school, there was an English teacher who almost *willed* me to write. I remember a writing competition in which I had placed as 'honourable mention' for two previous years. This was my last chance; I wanted badly to win. So I worked hard, wrote my composition, carefully typed it and coolly handed it to her one day before the deadline. I considered it a masterpiece.

She read it carefully. It was about the American revolutionary war and included descriptions of fighting. Finally, she placed the pages on her desk, looked at me, and said it was *well* written, but not really excellent or representative of what I was capable of doing. Why, she asked, couldn't she *see* the blood I wrote about, *smell* the sweat of men in battle, or *hear* the shouts and cries of dying soldiers?

In that moment I sharply hated her. I had failed and she was my scapegoat. I would show her. She would see blood, smell sweat, hear cries. I sat up through the night, writing with a new fury, feeling my words and moulding the structure of the composition with passion and discipline. Somehow, I had it typewritten and ready for the deadline. Yes, I won first prize. But I worry now, for I realize I was undoubtedly cocky (or insecure) enough to assume the triumph was *mine*. I wish I had been better able to articulate gratitude to her and sense the collaboration which the prize represented. She had led me through roadblocks within myself, and in the very act of exposure and vulnerability, she let me take a step towards expression.

17

Nothing less is required than a real entering into the lives of other men – into the very substance of their human experience in everyday living, into their language and the values to which they subscribe, into the experienced tensions of their very souls.

From 'A Theological Reflection on the Work of Evangelism'

18

While public opinion and the personal attitudes of whites concerning the Negroes were being formed by politicians and newspapers, there appeared in 1900 a book entitled *The Negro a Beast*, published by the American Book and Bible Society. The publishers of this book stated in the preface that if this book were 'considered in an intelligent and prayerful manner, that it will be to the minds of the American people like unto the voice of God from the clouds appealing to Paul on his way to Damascus'. In order that the American people might be convinced of the scientific nature of the 'Biblical truths' presented in this book, the author included pictures of God and an idealized picture of a white man in order to prove that white people were made in the image of God, as stated in the Bible, and a caricature of the Negro showing that he could not have been made in the image of God. This book had a wide circulation, especially among the church-going whites, and helped to fix in their minds, as it was argued in the last chapter of this book, that the Negro was not the son of Ham or even the descendant of Adam and Eve, but 'simply a beast without a soul'.

From 'Black Bourgeoisie' by E. Franklin Frazier

19 *Student Resolution*

Don't reform the world *after* graduation. Reform the university *now*: Drag the curriculum into today's world, make rules for humans instead of cogs in an academic machine, let students practise democracy on the campus. Don't wait until New Year to make the resolution.

20

I become increasingly impatient with the bigots and fence-sitters in my town. It is so tempting to think of myself as knowledgeable and 'liberal', and to be disdainful of my 'uninformed', prejudiced neighbours. How often these last few weeks I have been reminded that I can only make an effective witness if I move forward in love, and stop discriminating against the uncommitted.

Letter from a housewife

21 *A Prayer*

I'm drifting, Jesus.

I'm just no longer sure what involvement is supposed to mean. I'm beginning to realize it doesn't always mean demonstration or activity or meetings planning more meetings.

It can mean quietness too, can't it? It can mean withdrawing, even, from kinds of frenzied activity. Lord, I feel it can mean sinking into deep silences, taking time for relationships without agendas or limits, feeling very sensitively, and communing with life instead of using it as a racetrack.

Anyway, Jesus, the fire is burning low under my life right now. The clock may stop for a little while. I want to be as involved now as much as ever before, with you and other persons and life, Lord. Help me, Jesus, so that in my drifting I can be working with you in faith and storing up love.

22

We all live temporary lives. . . . We think that just for now things are going badly, that we have had to adapt just for now, and will start someday. We prepare to die with the complaint that we've never really lived. Sometimes I'm obsessed with this idea. You live only once, and for this one time you live a temporary life, in the vain hope that one day real life will begin. That's how we exist. Of those I know, I assure you, no one thinks that what he does every day is anything but temporary. No one is in a position to say, 'From now on, from whatever day this is, my life has really started.' Even the ones who have power and take advantage of it, believe me, live on intrigues and fear. And they're full of disgust with the prevailing stupidity. They live temporary lives too. They're waiting just like everyone else.

From 'Bread and Wine' by Ignazio Silone

23

I find myself interested in the theatre and its possibilities. Last spring some of us invented and method-acted a play for the other sisters, with very great success and satisfaction. Now one of the classes in our college has picked up the idea and is doing such a play as a project. We hope the plays are saying something. We know the method itself communicates a real sincerity and in-touchness-with-reality, since no prefabricated answer is possible. Kind of what we need on more levels of our living together.

Letter from a nun

24

To a close friend:
You know where I've failed? (I'm sure you do.) In not being able, quite correctly and circumspectly, to be very, very angry on occasion – at a person or thing or a happening – and in keeping this anger tame, lukewarm and placid.

But does anger mean hatred or just the opposite – involvement? Then *could* anger be a form of love, while indifference is not?

And I've failed in not being a 'nice' person – even, subdued, predictable, gentle.

Evenness. But in this moment I am depressed almost to the point of craziness. I am in one of those manic, seesaw, severe *down* moments before I come up again (for air, for light, for people). Always I come up, but this doesn't lessen the agony of the down moments, with their illogical strain of loneliness and pain. You are not so manic as I, and don't swing quite so far up and down. Yet I know you understand the strangeness of the highs and lows.

25 Wet Notes on Religious Movies

'... ['*Boy's Town*'] is a tear-jerker of the first water.' ('*Variety*')

'The picture ['*Fighting Father Dunne*'] has a touch of everything – hokum, humour, melodrama and tear-jerking sequences.' ('*Hollywood Reporter*')

'The picture ['*The Miracle of the Bells*'] is so weighted with mawkish melancholia that it drips all over the screen.' ('*New York Times*')

'Utterly and completely unrelieved in its lachrymal melancholia, '*The Miracle of the Bells*' is not entertainment – either cheerful or otherwise. Its direction is unimaginative, its performances undistinguished, and the whole picture is drenched in a kind of synthetic and sanctimonious piety that marks its pretensions to spiritual uplift as merely shallow and ridiculous.' ('*Cue*')

26 Cocktail Party in the Most Fashionable Big Downtown Hotel

An important ad agency is footing the bill. Photographers are all over the place snapping pictures for Negro publications. A big client – he is white – is hosting the party to introduce a Negro vice-president, show Negroes that the company is black-conscious, and make a big pitch for the Negro market.

'We're hoping for a spread in '*Ebony*', says a white P.R. man. 'The company is going all out, is prepared to do anything, to move into the coloured market in a big way.'

There is a Negro newspaperman at the bar. 'Christ, this is

swinging, isn't it?' he says. 'Drinks are on the house, they're feeding us steak dinners and I understand they're giving us some presents. I mean, this is *swinging*, man.'

27

I am going to be married to a guy who is at present serving a prison sentence as a C.O. I'm about as middle class as a person can get, and am fed up with religion and church clubs. But he is seriously considering the ministry, and going into a seminary when he's out of prison. I am faced with the probability of being a minister's wife. It may not sound like much, but it means a lot to find out that God lives in pads as well as in a gold-plated altar house. (Yes, I'm scared, too.)

Letter from a university student

28

The bodies of about 8,000 Viet-Minh troops and of over 2,000 French Union troops are buried in the reddish earth of the valley of Dien Bien Phu.

But no imposing monument, either French or Viet-Minh, honours the 10,000 men who died here and who may have done more to shape the fate of the world than the soldiers of Agincourt, Waterloo, or Stalingrad.

From 'Hell in a Very Small Place' by Bernard B. Fall

29

We're having a difficult time at my school, which is located on the North Side – lily white, upper middle class section of the city. We want to be involved in the social problems in the city – slumism, segregation in housing, bad schools – but little encouragement springs from the faculty. Oh, we do hold the meticulously organized 'interracial conferences', but they seem like a farce when only fifteen Negro students attend our school out of a student body of 1400.

Religion has no substantial correlation to my life at the present time, mainly because I can't adhere to the senseless legalities and constrictions of Catholicism. Most priests I know are the types who run around in cassocks and utter pious platitudes. I know what Tillich said about the 'freedom of faith' but it hasn't entirely actualized for me. I don't want to embark on a theological discourse because I probably sound like a typical irrational teen-ager. You know, God was always the anthropomorphic being in the long white robe and beard who sometimes came down from the sky to increase my weekend allowance.

Isn't it a greater 'sin' to appear physically in church and refuse to participate mentally and spiritually?

Letter from a high-school student

30

The dichotomy which some people resolutely set up between 'priest' and 'man' is incomprehensible to me.

Someone was telling me about a columnist who simply refused to meet me because he was 'confused' about me. (I couldn't understand how a meeting might stand in the way of clarification.) He said: 'He should either be a priest *or* an author.'

The dilemma. The columnist refused to see me as a human being but only in a role. Apparently he even wished to choose that role. I couldn't help but wonder about his 'image' of a priest: Cardinal Spellman? James Kavanaugh? Or maybe it would come from a screen portrayal by Montgomery Clift or, say, Pat O'Brien? Could the 'image' come from a guy in a church around the corner from where the columnist lives?

The columnist has locked me inside a Warsaw ghetto. I can only come out in whatever chains he chooses to give me. *He* will define 'sincerity'. *He* will define 'motivation'. *He* will define 'propriety'. *He* will define 'vocation'.

Maybe, since he seems to be playing God, he ought to define 'God'. But does he *know* God? Has he *met* God? This columnist is absolutely dogmatic about defining men and women whom he has not met. Does his dogmatism extend to God – or does he let God be free?

31 *Autumn Day*

I am growing older.

Such weird symbols – the smell of burning leaves, suddenly brisk winds, announcements of a Thanksgiving dinner and a Christmas wedding. Another year passed so quickly, too quickly.

Have I, simply and finally, lost all control? Is my life careening madly down a speeding track?

I must stop and think before Thanksgiving. I must examine my life before Christmas. I must make a resolution upon a red leaf.

NOVEMBER

I

My, the neighbourhood is bustling this morning.

Why? What's got *into* people?

That man carrying a briefcase is running (did he just rob a bank?). A man and a woman on the steps over there are almost to the point of making love in public (what has *happened* to our morals?). The man driving a bread truck is so hopped-up he nearly collided with the man driving a milk truck (at least, that would have been a healthy crack-up, ha, ha).

A special-delivery letter is being delivered to the house across the street (*nothing* ever happens to them, I must try to find out what this is about). Two plumbers just drove up to the apartment house halfway down the block (I swear, that place will simply cave in one of these days).

A liquor delivery man, on a bicycle, is tearing down the street (those society women drink gin, I hear, *before* lunch). A well-dressed woman is nearly flying along the sidewalk (*whom* is she meeting?).

Sitting here, observing all this, is absolutely exhausting me. What has got *into* everybody?

2

All of my life I have heard my ministers pray for boys and girls in love, the marital institution, for husbands and wives; but never for 'the two men who live and love together on the next block'. To have been recognized for the first time in a church as also a prize of God, was the single most God-sent moment of my public worship life.

Letter from a church member

3 'Despite the Fact That Your Face Is Black'

'I want you to know that *I* know your soul is white,' a white man addressed a Negro during a discussion of 'race relations'.

4

I remember when I suddenly found myself anti-white.

I couldn't bear the polished white smile over polite double-talk. For me it was all simply *white* versus *black. Goddam* white, *holy* black. Then I discovered how the question is not so much racial as *have* versus *have-not*. Yes, black America is, with the exception of the so-called black bourgeoisie, have-not. But a hard core of whites is part of the American have-not culture. And the Negro middleclass has been even more removed from the black ghetto than whites in the freedom movement. 'Niggers and beatniks' is the descriptive phrase used by some middleclass Negroes for blacks *and* whites.

At first, I very seriously called it the integration movement. I thought that was the point. I was acting paternalistically to 'help Negroes'. What a devastating moment of truth awaited me! *I* needed help. *I* wasn't free, for I dwelled in a nation where freedom was not yet a reality, but only a goal.

5 'We shall Overcome'

Now it's as awful as all those *other* hymns.

6 My Roof Is About To Cave In

Literally.

It's been raining hard for two days, and the old roofing is faulty. The roof men – I guess that's what *these* specialists are called – are fiddling about up there now.

It's an odd, odd feeling of insecurity. One's *roof* is shot (along with American foreign policy, the glory of the British Empire, civil rights, Indian nonviolence, Hollywood films, and the general state of morality). Is nothing sacred? Can't a man even account his own home (pardon me, flat) as his castle and preserve?

I can hear the roof men walking around. Storm clouds are gathering in the sky. It will surely rain again before they can complete their work.

I meant to rent a flat, not Noah's Ark.

7

Somebody has just called *another* conference, to be held in the usual luxury hotel in Washington, to discuss the gnawing Problem of Poverty.

Workshops and discussions about hunger and the poor will take place between the finest meals. ('Aw, I'll just take the sirloin, medium-well, and, yeah, salad with roquefort dressing.')

And, if there's any grass-roots show of genuine controversy or revolt, the planners can always ring in the President or a Government stand-in for a last-minute snow job to cool everything down.

After all, let's not move *too quickly* on Prickly Problems like Poverty. But a Prickly Pear might be nice.

8

Cusins: Do you call poverty a crime?
Undershaft: The worst of crimes. All the other crimes are virtues beside it; all the other dishonours are chivalry itself by comparison. Poverty blights whole cities; spreads horrible pestilences; strikes dead the very souls of all who come within sight, sound or smell of it. What you call crime is nothing;

a murder here and a theft there, a blow now and a curse there: what do they matter? they are only the accidents and illnesses of life; there are not fifty genuine professional criminals in London. But there are millions of poor people, abject people, dirty people, ill fed, ill clothed people. They poison us morally and physically, they kill the happiness of society; they force us to do away with our own liberties and to organize unnatural cruelties for fear they should rise against us and drag us down into their abyss. Only fools fear crime; we all fear poverty.

From 'Major Barbara' by George Bernard Shaw

9 'What Do I Think of the Church Now?'

A Negro, who had faced death threats, beatings and jail during his long search for freedom, was speaking. We were sitting in his living room in a small town in the Delta region of Mississippi.

'I don't know exactly,' he continued. We sat for a few moments. Finally, he spoke again. 'It is like the salt has become useless. We see churches which have beautiful buildings but are afraid to tell the truth.'

10

Like pillars of basalt the dead stood there, pressed upright in the chambers. There was no room to fall or even to bend. Even in death one recognized families. They still held hands, embraced tightly in death, so that it was difficult to tear them apart to clear the chambers for the next charge. They threw out the bodies, wet with sweat and urine, smirched with faeces, menstrual blood on their legs. Children's bodies flew through the air. There was no time. The riding whips of the Ukrainians flailed the working detachment. Two dozen dentists opened the dead people's mouths with hooks, looking for gold. Other dentists broke the gold teeth and crowns out of the jaws with pincers and hammers. Some workers searched the genitals and anuses for gold, precious stones, and valuables. Wirth called me over: 'Just lift this can with gold teeth, that's only from yesterday and the day before. You won't believe what we find every day in gold and precious stones.'

From the sworn testimony of SS battalion chief Kurt Gerstein, in 'The Nuremburg Trial'

II

In the meantime there are bills to be paid, machines to keep in repair, irregular verbs to learn, the Time Being to redeem from insignificance. The happy morning is over, the night of agony still to come; the time is noon: when the Spirit must practise his scales of rejoicing without even a hostile audience, and the Soul endure a silence that is neither for nor against her faith. That God's Will be done, that in spite of her prayers, God will cheat no one, not even the world of its triumph.

He is the Way.
Follow Him through the Land of Unlikeness;
You will see rare beasts, and have unique adventures.

He is the Truth.
Seek Him in the Kingdom of Anxiety;
You will come to a great city that has expected your return for
    years.

He is the Life.
Love Him in the World of the Flesh;
And at your marriage all its occasions shall dance for joy.

From 'For the Time Being' by W. H. Auden

154

12 Community

Think of the working N.B.C. communications centre with a thousand monitors being on tap and all your information coming in . . . live, film, and recorded, et cetera . . . edited, indexed, collated, cross-indexed, and the index operated cybernetically with electronic push buttons, so that you can get the stuff just like *that* when you want it! You know. Something happens in Athens. *Boing!* The guy pushes the button 'Athens', and the lights begin to blink all over the place as Athens starts pouring in.

Thomas Whiteside, 'The Communicator', an interview with Sylvester L. Weaver in 'The New Yorker'

'Are our city fathers aware that the decaying bodies of these rodents constitute a grave danger to the population?' The manager of the hotel can talk of nothing else. But he has a personal grievance, too; that dead rats should be found in the lift of a three-star hotel seems to him the end of all things. To console him, I said: 'But, you know, everybody's in the same boat.' 'That's just it,' he replied. 'Now we're like everybody else.'

Albert Camus, 'The Plague'

A fair, shaggy head came up over the edge of the bank, then shoulders, then arms. Someone was climbing up the cliff path with a bucket of water and seeing the doctor, he stopped, still visible only from the waist up. 'Would you like a drink of water? If you won't hurt me, I won't hurt you.'

Boris Pasternak, 'Doctor Zhivago'

We find how our neighbours think by consulting the results of the Gallup Poll. Our ideas, like our food, come individually wrapped, and sterilized.

John Hotchkiss, 'The Battle for Men's Minds', 'The New Statesman and Nation'

Don't worry, God says, you have gained all,
While men came in to you,
I, your Father,
I, your God,
Slipped in among them.

From 'Prayers' by Michel Quoist

13 *A Prayer*

How can we talk so much about love, Jesus, and refuse to love?

How can we claim to follow you while we fight wars, bomb cities, murder children, torture innocent people and wipe hope from human eyes and minds?

Are we going to just go on, Jesus, killing and killing until none of us will be left here? You know how human we are, Lord, because you shared our humanness with us. What can we do, with our humanness, to love and not hate each other, Jesus?

14 *At the Flicks:* A Hard Day's Night

Laugh, and the world laughs with you.

15 *Dry Notes on Religious Movies*

The hunk of Man looked hurt. He said cunningly: 'Haven't you seen my pictures? Didn't you see me push down those pillars with my own two hands in '*Samson and Delilah*'? Didn't you see me fight the tigers with my bare hands in '*Demetrius and the Gladiators*'?

'Yes,' I said, 'but I could probably have pushed down those pillars myself. Under the direction of Cecil B. De Mille.'

Mr Mature grinned. 'I guess maybe you could have,' he said. Victor Mature is a man of whom it could be said that he was saved by the Bible. Biblical epics like '*Samson and Delilah*' have kept him in the top category of Hollywood stars.

'Evening Standard'

Religion triumphant over paganism. And the soul is stronger than the flesh. Religion gets the breaks [in '*The Sign of the Cross*'], even though its followers all get killed in this picture. It's altogether a moral victory. . . . Neat, deft, and probably beyond reproach is the manner in which the scarlet punches are inserted. Every sequence in which religion wins out is built upon lurid details. The censors may object to the method but they can't oppose the motive, and in the way '*Cross*' was produced one can't be in without the other. . . . Appealing to another class is the sequence in which March finds himself unable to arouse Miss Landi. So he has a lesbian brought in who proceeds to supply what March lacks. No mistaking of what's going on. The sequence runs 500 feet.

'Variety'

16

My mother finds fault with everything I do. Whether I do something well, she contrasts it with the many things I don't do. And the more I try, the worse everything turns out. What can I do?

Letter from a teen-age girl

17 *Publicity Is Her Trade*

She knows little about human relations, for that is essentially *human* relations. Her blood turned into a lukewarm soft drink some time ago.

The telephone is her stock in trade. The soft, purring semi-voice performs her tasks, exploiting people to sell products, hour after hour. The phone cuts down human contact.

She has no cultural or political opinions, or else has buried them so deep that you'd find the gold at Fort Knox first if you started digging. Not that she can't be a bitch if a client gets out of line by presuming to be a human instead of a cog in a publicity machine. Pow! Then the purr becomes a hiss. But Mother Earth can quickly reward an errant child with a sunny smile if the child has conformed.

Essentially amoral, she concerns herself with surface morality. Although anti-Semitic, she publicly excoriates four-letter words. While hating Negroes, she wants sex (in conversation) handled with kid gloves. A religious traditionalist of the superstitious brand, she cannot bear the sweating Jesus or the virile Christ.

She's locked up inside something. It isn't within her*self*, for she's constantly denying humanness. She's too busy to concern herself about such questions this morning, anyhow. She's talking on the phone with an editor of a top woman's magazine and must hurry because she's going to have lunch (vodka, not gin) with a TV programme executive. She's considered absolutely tops. And she's fooling everybody.

18

I am seventeen years old. I am a Catholic. Sometimes I think that it surely will be nice when you can say, not 'I am a Catholic' or 'I am a Lutheran', or 'I am an Episcopalian' but 'I am a Christian', and you can say it with pride always.

There are eleven kids in my family, and I'm the third oldest. My dad is the man of the family and he and my mom talk just about everything over. Sometimes they just talk with their eyes. Us kids call it 'eye language'. I guess I'm a pretty lucky kid. I think about everything: boys, sex, friends, food, swimming, getting a job this summer, death, life, segregation, birth, flowers, the sun, friends who are getting married because they 'have' to, people who aren't as lucky as I am. People in general are the biggest occupation of my life, and I guess that makes me a pretty lucky kid, too.

Boy, I just wrote this letter to say hello, and look at the book you're getting from me. Sorry, I got carried away. Maybe you won't even read this letter, it sounds like you get pretty many of them, but I thought, you might appreciate a happy one for a change, because life can get pretty depressing sometimes.

Letter from a high-school student

19

It is a brilliant, very, very sharp, biting, alert autumn morning.

The wind is harsh and it will soon be blowing snow. Leaves rest in great heaps on the street corners and in front yards. There is no rest; everything points towards something; it is a bridge time, transitory, a moment braced by great stimulation but heavy with foreboding and melancholy.

There is so little time before – what?

20

I've learned something about what it means to be a Christian – this awful God-in-us awareness; this terrifying loving, opening, sharing; this painful *seeing*; this *being for* others; and perhaps, hardest of all, this letting others *be for* us, love us, give to us, *see* us.

Sometimes I get so frightened and want to run away – and sometimes I do – sometimes it's 'God! go away – I don't want you; stop reminding me – You, with your patch-of-blue skies and needing faces. . . .'

But if I have learned something of pain, I have also been filled with – flash of insight – 'YES' – Alleluia! Death and Resurrection – paradoxically inseparable – mystery, call to faith and love. . . .

Letter from a church member

21

It's one of those funny nights when the phone won't stop ringing.
Nashville is calling. New York. Los Angeles. Atlanta.
Seattle. St. Louis.

I had had some other plans for this evening, but the ringing
phone has changed them. And it's great. This is the rhythm
of life tonight – community is expressing itself all over the
place – so ring, damn it. Human beings can talk, relate, share,
cry, shout, inform, plan – you know, make it.

22

What about the hippie idea? Live simply, and peacefully.
The half-dozen hippies I know (really dedicating themselves,
not dressing a part) are strong believers in God, without a
thought of the church picnic.

Letter from a university student

23 *The Buttons World*

Make love, not war

APATHY
Hire Negro Clergy NOW
The Ghetto Must Go
  renewal
NO!
  HUELGA

24 *Thanksgiving*

What a downright curious day *this* has become.

It used to be so simple. Red-blooded Americans would shoot
a couple of turkeys and Indians, retire to their antiqued shacks
out of a Bergdorf-Goodman Thanksgiving Day ad in the *New*

York Times, sip ale (or *didn't* Puritans drink, and *were* Pilgrims also Puritans?), and prepare those great supermarket feasts.

Someone (no doubt the Paternal Figure, long since gone from our lives) would lead everybody in prayer, and as the people smelled the oyster dressing, piping hot roast turkey, and assortment of home-grown vegetables, they would *thank God.*

Now one can't go out and shoot either a turkey *or* an Indian: only Vietnamese, United States presidents, families of nine living in isolated rural areas, and ghetto blacks. Our days seem so complex, and many would have no idea what it really meant to *thank God* (it might seem particularly absurd if one considered God *dead*).

Thanksgiving requires some serious thought.

25 *A Middle-Aged Negro Woman in Mississippi*

is recalling her childhood, and how she and her other friends were not permitted by the white manager to attend the cinema in their home town. Films were for whites only. But one of her classmates looked white. She had blue eyes and light hair. So the other girls would pool their money and the 'white' Negro girl would go to the films. Then, during the lunch recess at school the next day, she would tell the rest of them the stories and how exciting everything was inside the cinema.

'We would gather around her,' the older woman reminisces. 'She was good and would relate the story step by step. But I think sometimes she developed a few plots of her own just to build it up more.'

26 *The Clouds in the Sky Outside the Jet,*

the ancient Greeks saw these too. A Greek sailor, philosopher or carpenter looked at the same formations: very

horizontal, alternating lines of light and dark; suddenly they
have changed to an ominous, sinister, but laughing-at-itself
form. Now, from the jet, I see something the ancient Greeks
did not see: another jet.

27 'You're Starting to Laugh White,'

the mother of a young Negro secretary employed by a white
firm cautioned her about the corrupting influence of white
values.

28

Now is the crisis in my life. I have just come to know the
meaning of fear, loneliness and despair. I am awaiting trial for
first-degree murder.

But I know I am not the only prisoner in the world, nor the
only person facing a situation in which there is little hope and
no dignity.

I'm not as alone in my 5 x 8 world as I was yesterday. I feel
I can cry for the world again instead of just myself.

Letter from a prisoner

29 *The Mother's Love*

Pity to the old mother, symbol of the soul of the nation
Her body is thin, similar to the form of our mother land
In her two brown eyes, two pearls of tears
The wrinkles on her forehead are like the ploughing lines of
    sufferings

Pity to the old mother whose heart is divided
One part is for Hai, her first son
One part is for Ba, her second son
She does not know among them who is Communist
She does not know among them who is anti-Communist

Her tears, shed by love have become a curtain
preventing her to distinguish red and blue
She only knows that her evenings are sad, very sad,
And that the blood of her first son is as red as the blood of her
     second son.

This poem by Tru Vu, Vietnamese Buddhist, is distributed by the Fellowship of Reconciliation

30 *My Country, Right or Wrong*

(But I prefer one world.)

DECEMBER

1

After some eight years of motion picture, advertising and television work in Hollywood, I decided, in 1951, to enter a theological seminary to begin studies towards becoming an Episcopal priest.

During my early seminary days, midterm exams were fast approaching. I felt discouraged, cold, dead tired, and hopeless about my ability to pass. After all, eight years in the communications industry was not exactly the academic life. If I had *ever* known how to study for exams, I was sure I retained little of that ability now.

It was a rainy, damp night in Berkeley, California. Shortly before midnight I drove from my seminary quarters to a near-by hamburger counter for a cup of hot coffee to help keep me awake for studying. When I turned on the car radio, a tune blared out. The noise of the falling rain and the din of my inner turmoil failed to drown it out. Ethel Merman was singing 'There's No Business Like Show-Business'. It was a funny, human, paradoxical moment. I got my cup of coffee, drank it, and drove back to the seminary to study most of the night.

2

Oh, I'd better hurry. I've got to get some seeds. I've got to get some seeds, right away. Nothing's planted. I don't have a thing in the ground.

Willy Loman, in 'Death of a Salesman' by Arthur Miller

3 *God*

Mrs Scott Smith, who owns a 170-acre grain farm near Warfordsburg, Pa., sums up the view of many farmers in the area: 'They ought to let God run the weather. He's always done a good job of it and always will. People never starved when the weather was let alone.'

From an article in 'The Wall Street Journal,' September 25, 1967

President and Mrs Johnson attended early services today at National City Christian Church, a half-mile from the White House. They heard the minister, the Rev. Dr. George R. Davis, deliver a sermon on 'What on Earth Is God Doing Now?' They also partook of communion.

Associated Press dispatch

4 Why We Are Here at the Greenville Air Force Base

Greenville, Mississippi, January 31, 1965.

We are here because we are hungry and cold and we have no jobs or land. We don't want charity. We are willing to work for ourselves if given a chance.

We are at the Greenville Air Force Base because it is Federal property and there are hundreds of empty houses and buildings. We need those houses and the land. We could be trained for jobs in the buildings.

What We are Demanding

1. *We demand food.* We are here because we are hungry. Our children can't be taught in school because they are hungry. They can't even get the food in school because they have to buy it and don't have the money.

2. *We demand jobs.* We are here because we have no jobs. Many of us have been thrown off the plantations where we worked for nothing all our lives. We don't want charity. We demand our rights to jobs, so that we can do something with our lives and build us a future.

3. *We demand job training.* We demand that people be trained for things that they want to do and that they be paid while they are being trained.

4. *We demand income.* We demand that poor people be given an income instead of handouts and food commodities. Until we get an income for our families, we want commodities which are fit to eat. The commodities we get now are old and full of bugs and weevils. We want fresh vegetables, fruits and meat. We want to decide what foods we want to eat.

The Federal government tells us to go directly to the state and county for help but when we go there they don't know what we're talking about.

5. *We demand land.* We are here because we don't have land. There are thousands of acres here that the government owns. We say we are supposed to be part of that government. We want the clear land and the unclear land and we'll clear the unclear land ourselves.

6. *We want 'Operation Help' to be stopped.* We don't want the Mississippi county boards of supervisors to have another chance to decide whether poor people should get food. We don't recognize these county boards because they don't represent us. We want the Office of Economic Opportunity and the U.S. Department of Agriculture to hire poor people we say represent us. We, the poor people want to distribute the food.

7. *We demand that Project Headstart schools be started now.* We demand that the Office of Economic Opportunity give us the money they promised us last September so that our children can be taught in Headstart Schools.

We are ready now to ask of President Johnson whose side
are you on – the poor people's or the millionaires'?

Poor People's Conference

5   The Business Man on Flight 28

aches with fatigue in his eyes and bones, body and nerves.

He wonders why everything can't stop just for an hour. He
can't stand thinking any more, at least not right now, about
problems, decisions and deadlines which pile up faster than
they can be met.

He yearns to get off the tightrope and razor's edge, out of the
fire. He wants a turn-off click to sound in his head. He is tired
of facing both an urgent need to get up in the mornings and an
urgent need to get to sleep at nights.

But the businessman knows he is deceiving himself. He
acknowledges that he couldn't stand the click which would
turn him off. He wants to be tired as a sign of being alive and
in the fight. He sees this as the price which must be paid for
living.

'I'm here, I'm alive,' he tells himself.

The plane lands. The businessman, clutching his briefcase
which contains the work he was able to do on the flight,
hurries to make an important phone call in the air terminal.

6

Would you like some human freedom with your coffee
this morning? Would you like some justice and bitters with
your gin?

7

This morning's newspaper is an editor's dream.

There were *three* major news breaks – one in London, the

others in Moscow and New Delhi. Too, there was a fascinating power play in the United States Senate, a charismatic foreign dignitary visited Washington, and a blonde film star eloped with a Detroit auto tycoon.

There was an important theatre opening and a first-rate film by an Italian director had its debut. A highly interesting memoir by a former United States cabinet member, containing sensational revelations of historical importance, was reviewed on publication this morning. A national golf tournament had a surprise winner who came from virtual anonymity to knock off all the well-known name players.

The first-page layout is stunning. The lead editorial is finally taking an unequivocal, and newsworthy, position on a question that's been bugging everybody. The cartoon is memorable. The humorist's column is his best in months. The local news feature is about an exciting educational experiment. The TV columnist got mad and finally decided to blast educational television for being gutless and getting into controversy.

Shouldn't today's paper be placed on exhibit in the Museum of Modern Art?

8

So, everyone is crying, begging and praying that we don't separate them and take their husbands and fathers, sons and grandfathers. The women wail and moan.

Then they watch in terror as we burn their homes, personal possessions and food. Yes, we burn all rice and shoot all livestock.

Some of the guys are so careless! Today a buddy of mine called 'La Dai' ('Come here') into a hut and an old man came out of the bomb shelter. My buddy told the old man to get away from the hut and since we have to move quickly on a sweep, just threw a hand grenade into the shelter.

As he pulled the pin the old man got excited and started jabbering and running towards my buddy and the hut. A GI, not understanding, stopped the old man with a football tackle just as my buddy threw the grenade into the shelter. (There is a four-second delay on a hand grenade.)

After he threw it, and was running for cover, (during this four-second delay) we all heard a *baby* crying from inside the shelter!

There was nothing we could do . . .

After the explosion we found the mother, two children (ages about six and twelve, boy and girl) and an almost newborn baby. That is what the old man was trying to tell us!

The shelter was small and narrow. They were all huddled together. The three of us dragged out the bodies on to the floor of the hut.

IT WAS HORRIBLE!

The children's fragile bodies were torn apart, literally mutilated. We looked at each other and burned the hut.

The old man was just whimpering in disbelief outside the burning hut. We walked away and left him there.

My last look was: an old, old man in ragged, torn, dirty clothes on his knees outside the burning hut, praying to Buddha. His white hair was blowing in the wind and tears were rolling down . . .

We kept on walking; then the three of us separated. There was a hut at a distance and my squad leader told me to go over and destroy it. An oldish man came out of the hut.

I checked and made sure *no one* was in it, then got out my matches. The man came up to me then, and bowed with hands in a praying motion over and over.

He looked so sad! He didn't say anything, just kept bowing, begging me not to burn his home.

We were both there, alone, and he was about your age, Dad. With a heavy heart, I hesitatingly put the match to the straw and started to walk away.

Dad, it was so hard for me to turn and look at him in the eyes, but I did.

I wish I could have cried but I just can't any more.

I threw down my rifle and ran into the now blazing hut and took out everything I could save – food, clothes, etc.

Afterwards, he took my hand, still saying nothing and bowed down touching the back of my hand to his forehead.

Letter from an American soldier in Vietnam

9 *Costumes*

Some of us were joking the other night about archaic religious dress and especially the enigmatic, round, white clerical collar worn by many clergymen. It communicates – but what?

The next day I was having a cup of coffee in a big hotel where there was a Shriners' convention. I noticed the men's cylindrical red hats, with black tassels and silver attachments. I thought to myself, 'How odd.'

Then I noticed some of the Shriners, in their hats, noticing me in my enigmatic, round, white clerical collar.

10 *What's This Space Thing?*

Will yellows and reds, blacks and whites, meet out there? Will they make it out there? If so, maybe they'll send missionaries back here.

Will the new space people use deodorants? Will they fight communism? Will they have film stars? Poets? I wonder what name they'll give God, and if they'll be right- or left-wing.

Will somebody build highways on Mars, ice cream shops on Jupiter, green-stamp redemption centres on Venus, white colonial churches on the moon and Freedom Houses on Saturn?

I hope each twinkling star won't be an arsenal.

II

My Sunday School teacher doesn't like the lessons our church provides because they deal with life and aren't Bible. Our lessons this quarter are on poverty, which I have become more and more involved in and concerned about. My teacher says her family once had it rough and they made it okay, so anyone who doesn't make it is a lazy bum. She doesn't want us to study poverty or talk about it, but just read the Bible. I disagree with many things she says. The other day I spoke my mind. Now she's angry with me. I just want to be able to give my opinion. I don't want the Council of Bishops to take action on my ideas to see if they are sound! Then I begin to think, why won't anybody let me go against the middle-class tradition?

We have Communion tomorrow and I don't really know whether to go or not. Are we sharing in the name of Christ in our everyday life? Can we share in 'grape juice and plastic' and not in life? I'm just a fifteen-year-old kid and you know today I don't even know where I am spiritually. The teacher says we should stick with the church the way it is and, when we have any questions, to get more involved in the church and they'll be answered. Which doesn't work. What happens is you become frustrated almost to the point of giving up altogether.

Letter from a high-school student

12

I wish every student could have the experience of being, at least once in his lifetime, a *foreign* student.

When I went to England and Europe for graduate study, I became alive in an altogether new way. Ideas, persons, concepts, wholly new equations rushed towards me; I was consumed by them.

During studies in Switzerland, my three closest friends were a Japanese, an Englishman and a Brazilian. We examined our own, and each other's myths about nationalism, religion, sex, society, politics, technology: It was a long list, and we would talk animatedly late at night, argue furiously, and alternate between accepting one another as human beings and as geographical symbols.

One night we had been in the near-by village, drinking the cheap wine of the region (a staple for students; Coca Cola was expensive) and talking. Walking back through the countryside, we entered an ancient stone chapel. It was past midnight, and the moon was shining brightly. There were many feelings buried deep inside us; we felt unable to let them out yet. That night, standing together in the old chapel, we began – quite spontaneously – to sing. At first tentatively, finding our way, then growing in volume, assurance and solidarity – we sang the Negro spiritual, 'Were You There When They Crucified My Lord?' Then we quietly left the chapel and walked back along the moonlit country road to our school and rooms.

13

One summer day in Mississippi, in a town which was a miniature hell on earth rent with bombings, fears and rumours, I walked into a local store to make a purchase. I was wearing my round, white clerical collar and black suit, and in that setting and moment in history, the clerical collar was the symbol of 'outside agitator'.

The white lady running the establishment didn't budge from her solid place behind the cash register.

'What do you want, *boy*?' she said, levelly, looking at me from behind great spectacle frames. (Communication!) It was a moment to be cherished, like a rose petal crushed inside an old Bible.

14

Letter from a young man from the plantations of Mississippi, after a showing of *A Raisin in the Sun*.

MY PHYLOISPY OF LIFE
(*A Rainsin the son*)

I've offden wounder and Quostion myself about life. Why dose man behave the way he dos? What is man prpose? Will he ever achived his prpose? Then I ask myself this, what is my prpose? Will I achived my prpose?

Then say my prpose is my clibm a mountain, after I've riched its highest peek what then. Does life end there. Then if life is to countenure then where shall I go. What will I seek?

Then out of my seeking what shell I find? What is life, is it just a 'dream that drys like a raisin in the son' are is it like an actor who never been on stage, but leave when lights are gone.

So I leave my quostion unanswer because I see myself without a future. For I am not a man, and yet I am a man.

And until I am twice a man, I'll seek my prpose.

And in the movie everybody had a dream, wonderful dreams, that 'dryed like a Rainsin in the Son'.

Homer Crawford
From 'Town and Country Church'

15

In the city, the morning mood and the late-afternoon mood are so different.

At 5:30 P.M., it's so really exciting; there's a choreography in the spontaneous, rapid, free movement of people, running to catch a subway or bus, meet a date, have a drink, move into the jungle of a parking lot; people may be tired, but they seem urgently alive; people may be bored with each other and desire privacy, but they seem so unselfconsciously, warmly related;

there is a tremendous sense of expectancy about everything – the work day may be over, but somehow life is starting up from scratch. Underneath everything – all the choreography, movement, restlessness, rush, relating – there is explicit, urgent, surfaced sex.

At 8:30 A.M., everything is beginning, but it seems to be over; there's a kind of frustration and fatigue in the rush; there's a deadness caused by the requirement to punch a time clock or be inside a door or behind a desk at a certain moment; coffee has become strongly sacramental, but, as in the case of all sacraments, is not magic; sex is implicit, very slowly stirring again. Expectancy? It seems to exist for 5:30 P.M.

16 *At the Flicks:* Dr. Strangelove

Dying is as much a scream as living.

17

Hollywood turns out so sadly for its dead. The glistening world of make-believe places black crêpe over its bright lights. The big applause machine shuts down. The great stars of yesterday and today – there are really so few of them – don their proper sombre clothes, fight tears from washing down celebrated faces and march in the choreography of the publicized, photographed Hollywood funeral.

After the service of an important Hollywood executive, I found myself chatting with an equally well known, distinguished figure in the Hollywood scene. 'You know, I hate Hollywood,' he said, as everyone waited for cars to be brought around by chauffeurs and as fans snapped photographs. 'Every night when I get home I pull down the shades to shut it all out. But I could never leave. We're the royalty of America. Automobile executives are kicked out of hotel suites to make place for us. Airlines hold a half-dozen reservations open for us on trips. We dine every day in the finest restaurants in the world. The press reports our every move when we want it to, and ignores us when we want it to. I could never leave. We're royalty.'

When Marilyn Monroe died, the Vatican City newspaper *Osservatore Romano* wrote: 'We cannot help but reflect that la Monroe is the victim of a mentality, of a custom, of a conception of life which makes one a symbol.' Miss Monroe, in one of her last public statements, commented on the fact that she had been used as 'a thing' instead of treated as a person. She said she did not wish to be 'a thing'. The Moscow newspaper *Izvestia* noted that her death 'transcended the limits of personal tragedy and acquired social reverberations'.

18

Good-byes, I find, are hard.

There was a wonderful, old, very lived-in house which I loved. I had sat in front of its fireplace past midnight, looking at the last red coals in that old-fashioned hearth. I had stood, in the morning, outside in its garden, seeing the sky through the branches of its great trees. Finally, it was stripped, empty, cold. I stood for a moment in one of its rooms, to say good-bye.

There was a tree at Oxford which had been alive when Charles I was King. The tree was a friend, and when I was leaving the university to return to America, I made a point of visiting it once more. Certainly, to say good-bye. I wondered if we would meet again, and I was confident the great, friendly tree would outlive me on this earth.

Yet human good-byes are the hardest.

19

This cocktail party is an *important* one: important people, important money, an important room.

There are three hundred characters here in search of an author.

The thirty-sixth character, entering the room, has looked out upon the sea of faces, and then observed a particular face. 'I acknowledge that perhaps I love, but I do not like.'

The one hundred and seventy-first character has just spotted the eleventh. But someone else is blocking his way. 'Hello, how are you? Good to see you.' He's got to get over to *that* side of the room where the eleventh character is standing. 'Excuse me, pardon me, oh, hello, yes, it *is* nice. I'm sorry, I have to see someone. I was just on my way over *there* . . . yes, maybe later.' One hundred and seventy-one has got to get over there fast if he's going to talk turkey with eleven. 'Hell, this place is so goddamned crowded it's hard to move at all. . . . Yes, another scotch and soda, please, thank you. . . . Henry! Hi! I didn't know you'd be here tonight! Listen, about that contract. . . . You did?'

Thirty-six has stopped a waiter for a martini. 'I can think more clearly after I have a cocktail. I'm tired and a cocktail will lift me up, give me a brace and get me started again. It will be a new life.'

Author! Author!

20 *Notes to a Young Writer*

I don't like your book. I believe the failure is one of nerve, deep in yourself. You are a young Negro writer, and at this moment within this society, that matters a terrible lot. It matters not just to other people, but to you. Last year you said you wanted to be considered a writer first and a Negro second. This year you say you want to be considered a Negro first and a writer second. Ultimately, it won't make any difference whether you are a 'Negro' writer, a 'Jewish' writer, a 'Polish' writer or an 'Indian' writer, unless you can write.

Admittedly, the publisher has not helped by promoting his

new 'Negro' find. As a result, you have been further ghettoized by his stupid promotion. Hear what the newest Negro author has to say! Masturbate with him, suffer with him, be black (in your white-suburbia fantasies) with him, ball with him, riot with him! So you are inside an iron stereotype which is tighter than the mask you wore before. You probably thought you could use the publisher just as much as he was using you. I think you were wrong about this unless the bread was worth it. In which case, you're a whore. (Okay, it takes one to know one.)

Anyway, this boxes you in again just when you might have been freer. It puts you in the zoo. Your blackness, it's great. Your black consciousness, it's beautiful. Your blackness being exploited for a buck, it's not beautiful. It doesn't make you blacker *or* more human.

Is the fury working out of you or do you still feel stifled by it? Remember, you used to tell me it was almost physically suffocating at times. I'm not to preach to you about this, for I have never learned what to do with fury. It comes and goes, and I try to be as hospitable as I can. But I can't let it take over, in fairness to the rest of me, as well as to others who walk innocently into the line of fire. From your book, I sense that fury is still moulding you instead of your moulding it. As an artist, damn it, you must mould. How does one mould fury? I suppose, first, by recognizing its worth and at the same time refusing to worship it. It's not an unattractive god, full of sound, colourful, explosive, and spawning images like thunderclouds and great howling waves.

21 *Collage*

Draw a Gothic cathedral on canvas, with two unmatching spires (copy Chartres) and a great rose window (use stones for this). Try to get the following lettering done in needlepoint and stretch it across the bottom of the canvas, punctuated by shiny new coins: 'In God We Trust.' We want colour in this, blues, reds, yellows. Place gargoyles on the cathedral (use slate, copy Notre Dame). Sketch a town square setting for the cathedral. Suggest an old inn on one side and a cobblestone road along the front. On the right side, print these words in medieval script: 'God is great, God is good, God lives in our neighbourhood. God! – Grace said before meals in American slum.' Place some trumpeters in medieval costume on the road. Paint some angels flying above them.

22 Did Anybody Ever Tell You

you have nigger lips? (*Laughter*)

23 Community of Scholars

The president of this college is no scholar. He raises funds in both a desperate and a half-hearted way, and can be trusted about as far as a minor-league Machiavelli. His basic problem is that he'd like to be a big-league one.

The faculty is split right down the middle, drawn and quartered. The better people got out last year (at least that's the accepted state-of-the-campus thesis).

Student government is asking for a voice in college decisions and a chance to talk over issues publicly with the administration. Unfortunately, most faculty wouldn't be caught dead reading the student newspaper, and consider student government a cross between sheer effrontery and a colossal bore.

Too bad 'community of scholars' isn't descriptive of *this* college. There's no community of anybody around here.

24 It's Christmas Eve

The big mistake we have made is to place it *back there*. We have made it ancient history instead of modern life. It concerns

178

angels, shepherds, Mary, Joseph and an inn keeper, but not us.

We have decided, too, to confine Christmas to Christmas. On December twenty-fourth, it has not yet arrived. ('Santa Claus does not come, Johnny, until tomorrow.') On December twenty-sixth, it is over. ('We've got to get the tree outside, sweep the room, and clean up. It's all over, dear.')

So we don't really let Christmas come at all. By its very nature, it cannot be contained any more than God can be bottled up inside a church building to be visited once a week for an hour, or Jesus can be invoked in prayer to act as a convenient magician on call.

Fortunately, despite the fact that we don't let Christmas come at all, it is here all the time.

25 A Prayer

It's Christmas again, Jesus.

So we're going to celebrate your birthday another time around. But are we aware you're *real*, Jesus?

I mean, do we honestly accept your humanness as well as your being the Lord? I don't think so. Maybe this is why we seem to be despising humanness pretty generally in our world right now.

Thank you, Jesus, for your life as a baby, a growing boy and a man. Thank you for respecting and loving our humanness so much that you have completely shared it with us.

And thank you for being real, Jesus. Please help us to understand what it means to be truly human and real, with you and the others we share life with.

'Silent night.' The nights I know, Lord, are noisy and frantic. Be there with me in the noise and confusion, will you, Jesus? Happy birthday – I hope it's okay to say that to you, Lord. Thanks, Jesus, for being our brother as well as our Lord.

26

A mother addressed her small child on a street:
'Never, *ever*, touch a stray dog.'
Lady, how do you define a stray dog?
(And, lady, a stray dog may need a touch more than any other dog.)

27

POW!
Get with it.
Faster.
Faster.
FASTER.
There's no time for dilly-dallying.

28

I am a Christian (and Episcopalian) by tradition but not really by conviction, not yet, anyway. I want to believe because I want someone to thank for the great opportunity of life and because I am filled with sin and ache for confession and forgiveness and because I am afraid to die. But I don't dare believe – I'm scared that it's all wishful thinking and too good to be true. And besides, to commit myself to Christ would bring such challenge into my comfortable, complacent life. I'm quite content with this earthly paradise as long as I keep very busy and don't think too deeply, and I'm not really sure that I have the guts to change.

Letter from a housewife

29

They are seated in the terminal of an airport. Some are waiting to meet planes, others to catch planes, a few are victims of
cancelled flights.

All of them are watching TV in the great central lobby of
the terminal.

'You might not get the money after you're married,' one of
the characters in the TV film is saying. 'Why not make sure
and get it *before*?' A male voice breaks over this dialogue,
announcing a flight departure. Immediately another voice announces a flight arrival at Gate 14. A woman's voice comes
over the PA, 'Would the party paging P. J. Harris please *re*-
page? Would the party paging P. J. Harris please *re*page?'

'I'm through,' says the man in the TV film. 'I've had it,
Marie, and I'm getting out of here for good.'

Watching the TV film seems easier, for the people who are
seated inside the air terminal this afternoon, than reading yet
another newspaper or magazine, or just sitting and looking at
nothing. Why don't they talk to each other?

30

During my senior year in theological seminary, I was, on
Sunday mornings, 'seminarian-in-charge' of an old mission
church in San Francisco which had never achieved parish
status or had a full-time priest.

The people there were remarkably kind to me. During that
year, I presented my first confirmation class to a bishop. After
the service, during which a group of youngsters was brought
before the kindly, elderly bishop for the traditional laying-on-
of-hands, all of us sat around a table in the church basement
drinking coffee and eating cake.

It had been a pleasant occasion. But, after everybody had
departed, and I was locking up the old church, suddenly I

cried. Many thoughts overtook me, including my own inadequacy to train the children properly, and, indeed, the frail, mundane, unrelated life of that little church to terribly real life in the great world outside its decaying walls.

I recalled, too, a Sunday morning in the church, not long before. At most, a dozen persons had comprised the congregation. Four of us, three young boys and I, formed the procession which marched down the centre aisle. One youngster, his robe almost tripping him, led the way and carried the cross.

The processional hymn was 'Onward, Christian Soldiers'. It staggered me. It caused me to glimpse the great, good humour and very real sadness, the glorious poverty and mad pomp of the whole thing, and, as I followed the three young boys down the aisle towards the altar, I was shaking, half laughing, half crying.

31 *New Year's Eve*

Nothing will be new.

Yet we may try again. We may look outside the ghetto of self, perceive other human persons, and choose – however tentatively – to relate to them at levels of humanness. We may decide that certain things in the world, including love and justice, matter even more than our own lives, and commit ourselves to them. We may resolve to serve instead of only being served.

We may search again – perhaps the object of this search is not at all far away, but just around the corner, or in the next room, or in this one – for the fresh, honest and true vision. Without it, we perish together instead of living.

New Year's Eve: We must not betray the vision.